FRANK LLOYD WRIGHT: ARCHITECT

AN ILLUSTRATED BIOGRAPHY

FRANK LLOYD WRIGHT: ARCHITECT
AN ILLUSTRATED BIOGRAPHY

ALEXANDER O. BOULTON
INTRODUCTION BY BRUCE BROOKS PFEIFFER

THE FRANK LLOYD WRIGHT FOUNDATION

RIZZOLI
NEW YORK

■

First published in the United States of America in 1993 by
Rizzoli International Publications, Inc.
300 Park Avenue South, New York, New York, 10010

Library of Congress Cataloging-in-Publication Data

Boulton, Alexander O.
Frank Lloyd Wright, architect : an illustrated biography / by Alexander
O. Boulton ; introduction by Bruce Brooks Pfeiffer.
p.   cm.
"Co-published with the Frank Lloyd Wright Foundation."
Summary: Traces the life and work of the twentieth-century
American architect who called his innovative ideas "organic
architecure."
ISBN 0-8478-1683-4
1. Wright, Frank Lloyd, 1867–1959—Juvenile literature.
[1.] Wright. Frank Lloyd, 1867–1959. [2.] Architects.] I. Title.
NA737.W7B68 1993   93-12188
720' .92—dc20   CIP
[B]   AC

Frontispiece: "Oasis," the Arizona State Capitol project, Phoenix, Arizona, 1957.

Quotations by Wright are from the following sources: pages 12, 22, 60, The Architect and the Machine (speech, 1894); pages 32, 44, Modern Architecture, Being the Kahn Lectures (published lecture, 1931); page 46, Two Lectures on Architecture (lecture, 1931); pages 48, 90, Architect, Architecture, and the Client (speech, 1896); page 62, The New Imperial Hotel, Tokio (*The Western Architect*, 1923); page 76, In the Cause of Architecture: Second Paper *(The Architectural Record,* 1914); page 100, Poor Little American Architecture (essay, 1930); page 111, In the Cause of Architecture I: The Logic of the Plan (*Architectural Record*, 1928).

Line adaptations are based on the following Wright works: pages 12 and 48, sketch for a cover design for *Liberty* magazine "Saguaro" project, 1926; pages 22 and 62, presentation drawing for a mural for the Midway Gardens, Chicago, Illinois, 1913; pages 32 and 100, Max Hoffman Residence rug design, Rye, New York, 1957; pages 38, 60, and 111, presentation drawing for stained glass windows for the Avery Coonley Playhouse, Riverside, Illinois, 1912; pages 44 and 76, design from the façade of the Cinema San Diego project for San Diego, California, 1915; pages 47 and 90, from a rendering of the Imperial Hotel, Tokyo, Japan, 1915.

Drawings and photographs were provided by The Frank Lloyd Wright Foundation except: pages 16–17 the State Historical Society of Wisconsin; pages 58, 59, 86, 94, 95 photographs by Paul Rocheleau; pages 78, 103 photographs by Alexander O. Boulton; page 80 Chicago Historical Society; page 115 photograph by Michael Freeman.

Edited by: Lois Brown
            Isabelle Bleecker

Design by: Christina Bliss
           Tad Beck

Printed in Singapore

CONTENTS

PRESS BUILDING PROJECT FOR THE SAN FRANCISCO CALL, SAN FRANCISCO, CALIFORNIA, 1912.

INTRODUCTION

In 1930 Frank Lloyd Wright wrote:

*Not only do I fully intend to be the greatest
architect who has yet lived but fully intend to
be the greatest architect of all time.*

While he may not yet be considered the greatest architect ever, Wright has been recognized by the architectural community as the greatest American architect of all time.

Frank Lloyd Wright fought for an American culture—one without European influences—that reflected this country's democratic principles, and he created an American architecture in which to sustain these ideals. When he first opened his own architectural office in 1893, his residential

Frank Lloyd Wright

designs were considered by the establishment as revolutionary—curiously "modern." He had, in fact, made a complete break with the traditional style of his time, with the "Victorian" style. Citing nature as his inspiration, he described his architecture as "organic"—growing from within outward. He further identified it as appropriate to time, appropriate to place, and appropriate to man.

Frank Lloyd Wright believed that a building should belong to the era in which it is built (just as Greek columns belong to ancient Greece, not to the twentieth century), that a building should honor the natural landscape and the environment, and that it should, above all, serve mankind.

Because he broke with all the traditions of the past, he was considered a "radical" by his fellow architects. But to him the definition of radical went deeper than simply being revolutionary:

> To the young man in architecture the word radical
> should be a beautiful word. Radical means "of the
> root" or "to the root"—begins at the beginning
> and the word stands up straight. Any architect
> should be radical by nature because it is not
> enough for him to begin where others have left off.

Although Wright was a dedicated American—an admirer of men such as Thomas Jefferson, Ralph Waldo Emerson, and Walt Whitman—his work was first recognized and his influence first acknowledged in Europe. But it wasn't long before the homes and buildings across America began to exhibit some of the basic characteristics of Wright's work: the open plan, the corner window, the carport, the use of steel, reinforced concrete, and plate glass. Today, his "revolutionary" ideas have been so thoroughly absorbed into our domestic architecture that most of us are unaware that they originated with Frank Lloyd Wright.

Wright is famous for such spectacular buildings as the Johnson Wax Administration Building, Fallingwater, and the Solomon R. Guggenheim Museum. But hundreds of less well-known residences, built for unknown people, remain testimony to his dedication to the American family and his efforts to define the American experience; to place people in an environment harmonious with nature, in buildings that would comfort and inspire.

Bruce Brooks Pfeiffer
Director, The Frank Lloyd Wright Archives

OVERLEAF: *THE SOLOMON R. GUGGENHEIM MUSEUM, NEW YORK CITY, 1959. MR. GUGGENHEIM REQUESTED A BUILDING FOR HIS MODERN ART COLLECTION THAT WOULD BE UNLIKE ANY OTHER MUSEUM IN THE WORLD.*

ZIGGURAT

ZIKKURAT

TARVEGITZ

"It is a great
thing to really
live, and we
only live by the
insight to keep
in touch with
the beauty of
our own little
world within
the great
world—for
every man's
home should
be that to him."

CHAPTER ONE
THE VALLEY OF THE JONESES

Eleven-year-old Frank Lloyd Wright had just fallen asleep when he heard a sharp rapping on the stovepipe that ran up through the floor from the room below. He rubbed his eyes and heard a voice call out, "Four o'clock, my boy, time to get up." He sat up in the bed in the low-ceilinged little room and stared out the single window that pierced one of the whitewashed, sloping walls. It was still dark out. "All right, Uncle James—coming," the boy called out. He shivered as he pulled on his shirt and denim overalls. He went downstairs, splashed water on his face, and stumbled out to the barn to begin his day's work. As a teenager, Frank Lloyd Wright began most of his summer days in this way, working on the farm, learning, as his Uncle James said, "To add tired to tired and add it again—and add it yet again." From April until he returned to school in September, Frank Wright milked cows; chopped and carried

UNCLE JAMES
LLOYD-JONES.

firewood; fed and watered horses, cows, pigs, sheep, and chickens, worked in the fields; and ran errands about the farm. By 7:30 in the evening he went to bed, to be awakened, it seemed to him, only a few minutes later to start all over again.

Years later Frank Lloyd Wright would say that the valley near Spring Green, Wisconsin, where his uncles' farms lay, taught him everything and that Uncle James was responsible for all that he later became. But during those years when Frank was making that difficult transition from being a child to being an adult, he did not always appreciate the little valley. Twice he ran away, only to be found and coaxed home by Uncle James or another of his five uncles. In his mind he ran away even more often. His family thought he was becoming too dreamy, too sensitive, as they saw the faraway look in his eyes. Sometimes Uncle James would recognize it and call out, "Come back Frank, come back."

Many years later Frank Lloyd Wright would run to the valley, rather than away from it, to escape from his daily life. It was, after all, a beautiful place. When Frank's grandparents on his mother's side, Richard and Mary Lloyd-Jones, came to the valley in 1844, they were struck by how much it resembled their native south Wales. Steep hills covered with wildflowers and berries framed the rolling landscape. Winding through the rich bottom land was a stream that slowly made its way to the Wisconsin River. Back then, the trout in the stream were so tame, they would nibble crumbs out of a person's hand. Passenger pigeons unfamiliar with humans would light in trees, and the boys in the family would knock them off the branches with sticks and stuff them into bags to bring them home to roast. In those days Indians still wandered through the hills and valleys of Wisconsin. Occasionally, in the middle of the night, the family would wake to the sound of the doorlatch clicking open. Without a word, an Indian would come in and lie down before the fire. In the morning, before the family rose, he would be gone without a trace. Days later a haunch of venison might be found on the doorstep—a thank-you for a warm night out of the cold.

Soon the Indians no longer visited, the pigeons disappeared, and even the trout learned to be more cautious, but the Lloyd-Joneses prospered. The valley supported the farms of Richard and Mary and their five sons and four daughters. For many years they were entirely self-sufficient, raising the food they ate; preserving fruits and vegetables; butchering pigs and cows, then salting and smoking them to last the winter; weaving and dyeing the cloth for their clothes; making soap; building houses.

The family was exceptionally close-knit. It had to be, for as beautiful as their valley was, it could also be deadly. A common cold, a broken bone, the cut of an axe could be fatal. The little cemetery next to the chapel in the valley soon began to fill with loved family members.

Mary Lloyd-Jones, it was said, knew without having to be told when one of her sons was hurt. More than once she sat up in bed in the middle of the night and told her husband of some new ill that would befall the family. One night she saw a bloody foot in her dreams, and the next day a neighbor brought her son Thomas to the farm in the back of his wagon. Tom had been clearing a trail in the thick woods and dropped an axe on his foot. He spent weeks recovering.

When son Jenkin Lloyd-Jones was with General Ulysses Grant at the siege of Vicksburg, Mary awoke from a dream. "I see a battle, and bullets flying! He's been hurt," she told her husband. And indeed he had been. Jenkin soon mended, however, and did not return to Spring Green until Richmond had been taken.

Richard Lloyd-Jones, the patriarch of the Lloyd-Jones clan.

Mary, who had given her maiden name of Lloyd to the clan of Lloyd-Joneses, was mourned for years after her death in 1870. When she left Wales she had taken with her a handful of seeds of her favorite flowers. Years later family members would watch to see where those flowers would blossom in the valley each spring. After her death, when the large family gathered for a photograph in 1883, an empty chair was placed next to her husband. She was still a presence in the family, even though her body had passed away.

Overleaf: The Lloyd-Jones clan at Richard Lloyd-Jones's farm in Spring Green, 1883. Frank Lloyd Wright's mother and father stand third and fourth from the right in the back row. Their daughter Jane is in front of them, and Wright sits to the right of his grandmother's empty chair with his sister Maginel on his lap.

The family, for that matter, was always much larger than anyone could count. Richard and Mary, their sons and daughters, and their wives and husbands, and their sons and daughters, along with boarders and workers, always made a family census difficult. Timothy, for example, the Welsh stonemason, was not related by blood but was like another uncle to the many children. He quarried the stone and built the foundations and chimneys for all the children's homes. Above each mantle he would carve the family emblem, /|\ , which signified the Welsh motto "Truth against the world."

Mr. Sweet, a hired hand, had worked so long for the family that when he grew too old to work, he was given a plot of ground of his own. He built a small house and planted a garden, and family members sometimes brought him food and gifts.

When all the members of the Lloyd-Joneses' extended family, plus their friends and neighbors, got together, the result was apt to be a spirited and

WILLIAM RUSSELL CARY
WRIGHT.

ANNA LLOYD-JONES.

noisy celebration. In the summer, picnics or house raisings were occasions for great feasts. Wagons were loaded down with roast pork, turkey and chicken, corn on the cob, tomatoes, cucumbers, wheat bread, corn bread, cheese, homemade preserves, cookies, gingerbread, cinnamon-covered Dutch rolls, sugared doughnuts, and apple and pumpkin pies. If the children were still hungry, they could wander off and pick fresh plums and berries from the hillsides.

On such occasions the youngest members of the family would often be called on to recite memorized pieces of poetry, or Uncle Jenkin would give a sermon that would bring tears to everyone's eyes. Crying seemed at times almost as common as laughter among the intense Lloyd-Joneses, but the tears would melt into music as the family ended their festivities by singing old Welsh hymns.

Anyone who married into the clan, especially if they were not Welsh, had a difficult time fitting in. Frank's father, however, when he first courted and then married Anna Lloyd-Jones seemed ideally suited to the ways and temperament of the clan. William Russell Cary Wright shared with the Lloyd-Joneses an enthusiasm for music, education and religion. He had studied medicine and law but soon dedicated himself to the ministry. Like many Easterners in the nineteenth century, he had followed Horace Greeley's advice to "go West, young man." He left his home and family in Hartford, Connecticut, and became an itinerant minister, sometimes supplementing his income by giving music lessons. He even composed several piano pieces that were published in his day. His son would later recall him composing at the piano or organ. William Wright would hold his old pen in his mouth as he struck the keys with his hands, then grab the pen, scribble the notes on paper, and put the pen back in his mouth. Soon he had drawn dozens of long black whiskers on his face.

Most of Frank's memories of him, however, were not so comical. The young Wright sensed that his father never had much affection for him. He described his father teaching him to play the piano, punctuating each mistake with a sharp rap on the knuckles with a pencil.

Many years later Frank would remember pumping the wooden handle of an organ's huge bellows while his father played Bach in church. Frank was in a dark chamber behind the instrument, and a tiny oil lamp shone on the gauge that indicated the air pressure necessary to keep the organ playing. As the piece of music reached its most tumultuous fortissimo, the boy worked for dear life to keep air in the bellows, knowing only too well what would happen to him if his strength should give out.

He looked forward to the long, softer passages when he could rest. In those moments he stopped, tears running down his face, entranced by the beauty he had helped to create. Then just as suddenly, he would again throw himself into his pumping as the music continued its triumphant progress.

William Wright may have been blamed by his young son, as well as his wife and the Lloyd-Joneses in general, for many things beyond his control. There was perhaps an unbridgeable difference in their temperaments. William Wright, at forty-seven when they married, was seventeen years older than Anna Lloyd-Jones. It was his second marriage. Also, William Wright was a Baptist and Anna and the Lloyd-Jones clan were Unitarian. This may seem a subtle distinction to those who are neither Baptist, nor Unitarian. But to Baptists who generally believe in the necessity of personal redemption to release oneself from the turbulence of a sinful world, and to Unitarians, who presume an essential harmony between spiritual and earthly realms, the differences between their faiths can be stark indeed.

Ultimately, however, the cause of the problems that arose between William and Anna were very earthly. William Wright was unable to earn a living, indeed often seemed indifferent to the whole idea of making money. This was not a rare problem in the latter half of the nineteenth century, especially for the sons of old New England families, who had been taught as children that earthly pleasures were the reward for moral virtues. As new commercial classes rose to the fore, and as industry expanded, those without specialized knowledge or skills often found that virtue alone would not feed their families or pay the rent. William Wright, perhaps, was one of the many victims of America's march into the modern world. He and his family moved about from town to town as he was appointed to first one failing church and then another. He was unable to find, as the Lloyd-Joneses had, that perfect place where work and love both resided.

For a time he preached in Richland Center, Wisconsin, where his son Frank was born on June 8, 1867. In the next dozen years, however, William, Anna and Frank moved first to McGregor, Iowa; then to Pawtucket, Rhode Island; then to Weymouth, Massachusetts; and finally back to Wisconsin, where the Lloyd-Joneses' many connections could help the struggling minister and his family. By now Frank had two sisters, Jane and Maginel, but his parents' marriage was slowly disintegrating from the many strains that had been placed upon it.

William Wright had an enormous influence on his son's life. Frank

Lloyd Wright's ability to translate between emotions and physical forms perhaps had its earliest training in those sessions when he pumped the bellows while his father played the organ. The son's continuing love for music, which played an important role throughout his life, was part of his father's legacy to him. Perhaps some of his wanderlust, and his financial irresponsibility, can be attributed to his father as well.

It was his mother, Anna Wright, however, who, more than any other person, directed the course of his life. Frank believed that even before his birth his mother had decided that he should be an architect. While she was pregnant with him, she cut engravings of English cathedrals out of a magazine, framed them, and hung them about the room that was to be his.

While visiting the Philadelphia Centennial Exposition in 1876, Anna Wright discovered the work of the German educational reformer Friedrich Froebel. Most famous today for having come up with the concept of the kindergarten, Froebel believed that there was a basic unity underlying the various aspects of a child's basic education. Early tactile experiences, he taught, could help foster abstract thinking. Froebel therefore devised a system of wooden blocks, spheres, and triangles, with colored paper of different sizes and shapes, that would turn child's play into a learning experience. Anna Wright bought the set of Froebel Gifts, as they were called, and when the family lived in Weymouth, she took trips into Boston to learn the new system of instruction. At home she would watch for hours as Frank played at a low mahogany table, its polished surface reflecting the bright colors and forms of the Froebel "toys." He would later build those fantastic shapes and patterns on a much larger and more permanent scale.

Frank Lloyd Wright's education was not solely in the visual arts. Reading aloud the literature of the New England poets and transcendentalists was a common part of the family's entertainment in an era without television. In the evening, when all the chores were done, the words of James Russell Lowell (a relation of Frank's father), Longfellow, Emerson, and Thoreau echoed through the rooms of the Wrights' and Lloyd-Joneses' houses.

The emotional tension between his mother and father was perhaps never resolved by Frank Lloyd Wright. Relationships established as a child and imprinted on one's mind do not simply vanish. Months after William Wright left his wife and family for the last time, Frank's sister Maginel was walking home from school and saw her father. He took her hand and brought her to a store in town, where he bought her a brightly colored hat and shoes, then sent her home. Anna Wright was not pleased by Maginel's new costume. She disliked hats and never wore one herself; she thought they were foolish and extravagant. The shoes were too cheap and gaudy. She took them from Maginel, opened the lid of the cast-iron stove, and placed them in the fire. Then she brought Maginel back downtown and bought her a new pair of French kid shoes. From such acts as these it would be a wonder if Frank, Jane, and Maginel did not learn some interesting lessons about style as well as about personal relations.

Frank Lloyd Wright's life in many ways was not unlike that of most other children. He was sometimes obedient, sometimes mischievous. He was sometimes shy, sometimes outgoing. He also experienced the pain that adults often unwittingly inflict upon those they love. However, his rich imagination, perhaps the birthright of all humans, was not fettered as it is in most of us. During the times when he was not on the farm, the boy had a room in the attic of a house his mother rented in Madison, Wisconsin. The smells of printer's ink, oil paints, shellac, and turpentine constantly drifted down the stairs, under and around the door that was marked with large capital letters, SANCTUM SANCTORUM. Behind that door he and a few childhood friends constructed bows and arrows, bobsleds, and fantastic kites, and invented catamarans, ice boats, and water wheels.

In every exercise of his fantasy, he was encouraged by his doting mother. She gave him the tools, physical and mental, that he needed to sort out the lessons in his life, to discover what was valuable to him and what he could discard. Ultimately, he did not toss away much. His imagination found ways to harness all the warring tensions around and inside of himself. His parents' conflicts, the hard work of the farm, his insecurities and pains, the warmth of the large extended family he found in the valley—he was able to imagine each as an individual part of his life, always changing, yet always a part of a larger pattern. Like his grandmother's flowers which grew by uniting the elements of air and earth, rocks and water, in the valley of the Lloyd-Joneses a little seedling took root that later would become a mighty oak.

FRANK LLOYD WRIGHT AT AGE THREE.

"The end and
aim of all good
education is to
make man more
alive to everything,
or in other words
to make everything
more keenly alive
to him, to make
'sermons in stones,
and symphonies in
running brooks'
an everyday
possibility."

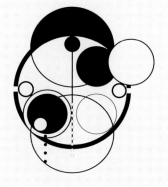

CHAPTER TWO

CHICAGO

Frank Lloyd Wright arrived at Wells Street Station in Chicago on a spring night in 1887. He was running away again, or was he running to something? In the drizzling rain at the train station, he saw electric lights for the first time in his life. He thought the dazzling, sputtering light was ugly. In his pocket he had seven dollars, the proceeds from pawning some of his father's books. He melted into the crowd at the station and walked with it to the Wells Street Bridge over the Chicago River. As he crossed, he heard a bell clang and saw the crowd run, then watched as the bridge, with him on it, swung out over the channel. A tugboat, puffing clouds of steam, slowly pulled an enormous grain barge through the gap as he stood transfixed.

Chicago in the last years of the nineteenth century was perhaps the most auspicious place and time for a young architect to begin his career.

The city was growing faster than almost any other in the world. Half a century before, it had been a small trading post on the edge of a wilderness. By the time Frank Lloyd Wright arrived, it was on its way to becoming the second most populous city in the nation. It had parlayed its unique geographical position between two great water systems of the continent into the nation's major transportation center. With the development of the railroad, Chicago became the final destination for the millions of head of cattle raised on Western ranches. From Chicago refrigerated boxcars quickly transported their meat to the growing cities of the East. The city was devastated by fire in 1871, but this only gave new incentive to rebuild it on vaster and more magnificent plans. At the same time that Chicago was rising from the Illinois prairie, new technological innovations allowed for the construction of taller and taller buildings. The elevator and steel-frame construction revolutionized the forms of city buildings.

The phenomenal growth of Chicago did not occur without its unique pains. As people poured in from practically all over the world, they brought with them new and sometimes impossible demands on the systems of supply and distribution. Social tensions flared up in 1883, when a clash between police and demonstrators in Haymarket Square left eight dead and almost one hundred wounded. A strike at the Pullman luxury sleeping-car plant eleven years later ended only after President Grover Cleveland sent federal troops to quell the uprising.

The anguish of the growing nation often found the heart of its misery in Chicago and the Midwest, but it also found there a group of individuals with new ideas and new plans to address the many problems that the country faced at the beginning of the twentieth century. Jane Addams, the social reformer, was one of these people. So too were John Dewey, the educator and philosopher, and Frederick Jackson Turner, the historian. They brought a new vision and, in their work, celebrated a native American spirit, born on the frontier, emphatically practical and individualistic, impatient with old rules and formulas, and openly critical of the cities of the East, with their antiquated philosophies, their corruption, and their commercialism. William Jennings Bryan focused much of this Midwestern outlook in his populist campaigns for the presidency in 1896, 1900, and 1908 and in his continuing isolationist and anti-war activities throughout his political career. The spirit of the Midwest was probably best captured, however, in the poetry of Carl Sandburg and Vachel Lindsay, who celebrated Chicago, the common people, and their native prophet, Abraham Lincoln. This was more than simply a new philosophy;

OPPOSITE: CHICAGO IN 1900, A FEW YEARS AFTER FRANK LLOYD WRIGHT MOVED THERE.

it was a way of life for many Midwesterners, and no one was more inspired by it, and would ultimately do more to spread its influence, than Frank Lloyd Wright.

For four nights after he arrived in Chicago, Wright lived in a rooming house on Randolph Street and wandered through the streets during the day, looking for a job. He was determined to be independent and not rely on his Uncle Jenkin, who now lived in Chicago and was becoming a famous Unitarian minister. Wright's new shoes pinched his feet and gave him blisters. By the fourth day he was down to his last twenty cents. Finally he visited the architectural offices of Joseph L. Silsbee and was hired as a tracer for eight dollars a week.

The young Wright was not totally inexperienced when he came to Chicago, nor was he able to make a complete break with his family ties. While he attended the University of Wisconsin, he had worked briefly for the professor of engineering, Allan D. Conover. In Wisconsin he had begun to draw architectural sketches and even assisted in the interior design of the small three-room chapel in the valley near Spring Green—a project sponsored by his Uncle Jenkin and designed by Silsbee. Wright's fall from the nest was a gentle one. When Uncle Jenkin heard his nephew was in Chicago, he found him a place to stay and often invited him over for dinner. For several months Frank Lloyd Wright worked in Silsbee's office, spending part of his time working on plans for buildings for his Uncle Jenkin and other family members.

One of Silsbee's projects was Jenkin Lloyd Jones's All Souls Unitarian Church. In many ways his church was like a part of the valley transplanted to the city. Jenkin Lloyd-Jones tended not only to the spiritual needs of his congregation but also to their social and educational needs. All Souls had a library and a kindergarten. In the evenings the church hosted intellectual and literary meetings and acted as an all-purpose community center. It was never closed. Jane Addams sometimes visited the church, and her own Hull House, which originated the settlement-house movement in the United States, had much in common with Uncle Jenkin's All Souls Church.

It was at a church dance that Frank Lloyd Wright first bumped into Catherine Lee Tobin—literally. They were both rushing across a crowded room, not looking where they were going, when they collided. Kitty, as she was called, fell to the floor, and the awkward Wright whirled around, seeing stars. He helped her up—she laughing; he apologizing; neither one realizing how fateful this small collision would be. He felt the bump on his forehead grow as he walked Kitty over to her parents and apologized again, and he was surprised when they invited him over for dinner the next evening.

Kitty was sixteen, three years younger than Frank, yet in many ways more mature and more practical. She was tall and pretty with red hair, and—as everyone knew—she was shamelessly pampered by her loving family. Wright was attracted to her perhaps as much for her strong will as for her obvious physical charms. Over the course of the two-year courtship that followed, both Frank's mother and Kitty's parents could see the affections of their children grow, and they feared that the youths were moving too quickly down a path that required some serious reflection. Kitty and Frank, however, were only more inspired by their parents' obvious misgivings and obstructions, and they became more and more infatuated.

At the same time as Frank was beginning his new life in Chicago and Uncle Jenkin was building his great new church, Wright's maiden aunts back in Spring Green were beginning their own venture. In 1887 Nell and Jane Lloyd-Jones opened Hillside Home School on land that had been given to them in their father's will. Like all Lloyd-Jones projects, its purpose and method were closely tied together. The aunts combined a home, a school, and a farm. Students, who came from all over the United States, learned by doing. They worked on the farm and studied history, mathematics, literature, and languages in a warm, family environment. All of the valley and the farms of the Lloyd-Joneses were part of the school. The students learned about animals and plants, and geology and geography, by observing the panorama of nature firsthand. Students soon knew all of the horses and cows on the farms by name. They could identify birds by their calls and plants by their seeds. On nice days they might go riding or on sleigh rides or picnics. They practiced music and drama, and always had an attentive audience in the many Lloyd-Joneses who attended, and sometimes participated, in their activities. Many of the family, for that matter, were on the school's payroll. One of Frank's cousins taught mathematics, and another was the gym teacher. His sister Jane taught singing and piano, and his mother, for a time, was a dormitory matron.

It was not surprising, then, that Aunt Nell and Aunt Jane asked Frank to design a building for the school. Silsbee gave him time off to supervise its construction. It was Frank Lloyd Wright's first project. Although unremarkable by the standards of his later buildings, the Hillside Home

School had a warmth and practicality uncommon for any architect's first endeavor.

Over the years Wright would design other buildings for his aunts' school, and it would grow into something far vaster than anyone then imagined. But the school looked backward as well as forward. Its leaves and branches might point toward the future, but its roots were firmly planted in the history of the Lloyd-Jones clan. Over the fireplace Timothy the stonemason placed the maxim "Truth Against the World," with the symbol ⁄⁄\ .

After working for Silsbee for several months, Wright joined the firm of Adler & Sullivan. This turned out to be one of the most important events in his career. Many years later Frank Lloyd Wright would still praise his great mentor, Louis Sullivan, as "the master for whose influence, affection and comradeship I have never ceased to feel gratitude." Wright forever called Sullivan his *Lieber Meister,* and described himself as merely "a pencil in the hand of the master."

Dankmar Adler and Louis Sullivan ran one of the most successful architectural firms in Chicago during the years that Wright worked there. Along with William Le Baron Jenney, Burnham & Root, and Holabird & Roche, they were among the major innovators of the Chicago school of architecture that virtually invented the skyscraper during the last decade of the nineteenth century. Replacing thick masonry walls with steel-frame construction and plenty of windows, they built the world's first efficient, as well as attractive, tall office buildings.

The skyscraper represented a social revolution as well as an architectural one. Advances in transportation coincided with the new building technologies. Streetcars, and later automobiles, brought workers from increasingly distant suburbs to travel by elevator to heights previously undreamed of. Old patterns of living and working close together were slowly replaced by a division of home and work that changed the nature of both the workplace and the family. Old architectural philosophies of design and construction, which had seemed adequate for thousands of years, in a stroke became obsolete as buildings reached ever-new heights. The purpose of a building could best be served by jettisoning the antiquated ideals of design. The new architectural motto, first announced by Louis Sullivan, was "form follows function."

Dankmar Adler and Louis Sullivan formed an odd couple, a Jew and an Irishman, markedly different in style and background. Their differences, when added together, brought them successes neither could have

FRANK LLOYD WRIGHT AND CECIL CORWIN, A FRIEND AND COLLEAGUE HE MET WHILE WORKING IN THE OFFICES OF JOSEPH L. SILSBEE.

achieved alone. Dankmar Adler was the astute engineer who could find the perfect solution to the most difficult structural problem. His art of bringing things harmoniously together included not just iron, steel, glass, and masonry but also people. He was a congenial and tactful businessman who could deal persuasively with clients and workers. For a while he was even able to establish an agreeable working relationship with the egocentric and irascible, but brilliant, Louis Sullivan.

Frank Lloyd Wright was "Sullivan's new man." Late at night Wright would listen for hours as Sullivan expounded his metaphysical architectural philosophies. Sullivan would continue talking, seeming to have forgotten that his pupil was still in the room, until finally Wright would excuse himself and take the last trolley home. Over the years the master would come to depend more and more on his youthful protégé. By the time Wright left, he had his own office next to Sullivan—and larger even than Adler's.

Wright loved Sullivan and admired his genius, but even he could see his fellow draftsmen cringe with fear whenever their boss walked by. Professionally, Adler and Sullivan were able to bring their immense talents together to create buildings that determined the course of American architectural history, but their conflicting temperaments had a disastrous effect on the men who worked for them. Quiet, groveling and servile when under observation, the draftsmen were resentful and hostile when they were by themselves and their anger was often directed at unsuspecting targets.

Wright's good relations with Sullivan did not help his relations with his co-workers in the drafting room. One day he was challenged to a boxing match by some of his colleagues. Perhaps it began innocently enough. Half a dozen of the men in the office were in the habit of going to the back room during lunch. They would take off their coats, vests, and collars and spar a few rounds as relaxation. But for Frank Lloyd Wright, few things were innocent and inconsequential. He accepted the challenge boldly. His work on the farm, along with boxing lessons in the city, had given him enormous confidence.

He pulled on his gloves—he would later remember being offended that they were soiled—and before his opponent had gotten up his guard, Wright struck him in the face. The man came after Wright, slugging away, without style or grace, and Wright let him slug—standing up to him, then backing away, continually drawing him on. One of the men shouted, "Time!" But Wright would not stop. He punched his rival again in the nose and drew blood. The two boxers crashed back and forth, the onlookers racing out of the way, knocking over everything that could come loose. Another man took the bleeding boxer's place, and Wright, incensed, rushed into him, pummeling him with punches. Finally the crowd separated the fighters. Wright knew he had won the boxing match and no one would challenge him again, but he had also lost. He had gotten angry, lost his temper, and made enemies of all his fellow workers. Wright's fighting in the back room at Adler & Sullivan was perhaps a minor incident, a youthful indiscretion, in a life filled with intellectual challenges and dazzlingly brilliant accomplishments. But the fighter in Frank Lloyd Wright never died.

"Human houses
should not be like
boxes, blazing in the
sun . . . Any building
for humane purpos-
es should be an ele-
mental, sympathetic
feature of the
ground, complemen-
tary to its nature-
environment,
belonging by kinship
to the terrain. A
house is not going
anywhere, if we can
help it. We hope it is
going to stay right
where it is for a
long, long time."

CHAPTER THREE

OAK PARK

The invention of the skyscraper created the modern city, and it also created the suburb. During the day the urban skyscraper housed people at work, who at night commuted back to their homes in the suburbs. Ultimately the bedroom communities would have new architectural forms comparable to that which dominated the city. This would be one of Frank Lloyd Wright's major legacies.

Frank Lloyd Wright, by this time, had lived in both the country and the city. His introduction to the suburb happened when his mother came to Chicago to join her son. Anna Wright moved to Oak Park, Illinois, where she worked as a housekeeper for a Universalist minister, and for a short time Wright lived with his mother and sister in the small community thirty minutes by rail from downtown Chicago.

THE H. J. ULLMAN HOUSE PROJECT,
A PRAIRIE HOUSE FOR
OAK PARK, ILLINOIS, 1904.

Wright and Kitty by now were seriously thinking of marriage, but they knew he could not support a family on his draftsman's wages. Frank went to Sullivan and explained the problem. From his office Sullivan called down the hall to Adler. They conferred for a minute and then made a proposition. They would give Wright a five-year contract with the firm, at the highest salary of any draftsman in the city, and Sullivan would give Wright a five-thousand dollar loan to build a house. Wright could pay the money back out of his monthly paycheck. It was a deal that made everyone happy. Wright quickly accepted, and Frank and Kitty were married shortly thereafter on a rainy Saturday in June 1889. His Uncle Jenkin officiated at All Souls Church.

The house that Wright built for himself and his wife on the corner of Forest and Chicago in the sleepy community of Oak Park was his first great ongoing experiment in architecture. It was to Wright a plaything, like a set of Froebel building blocks, to be put together and taken apart and put back together again as many times as he liked. He was never finished constructing and reconstructing it. As the house now stands, it has been marvelously restored by the National Trust and the Frank Lloyd Wright Home and Studio Foundation to appear much as it did at the turn of the century, when Frank and Kitty Wright raised six children within its walls. But a visitor should remember that, as accurate as the restoration is, it can never reproduce Wright's own feeling for the first home he owned. Today it now has an aura of permanence and stability that it probably never had for Wright.

During those years the Wrights' house and family were continually growing. In its earliest form the house looked like a seaside cottage, inspired by the shingle-style mansions designed by H.H. Richardson and others on the Atlantic coast. It had, however, a playful relationship to the classical forms that Wright would later criticize so harshly. A large triangular gable, apparently supported by two semioctagonal bays, mimics the stark geometry of a Greek temple. In the gable a Palladian window, its proportions stretched almost beyond recognition, suggests Frank Lloyd Wright's tongue-in-check homage to classicism.

These were extraordinarily happy and productive years for Wright. Just as in the valley, Wright was surrounded by a large and affectionate family. His mother and, for a while, his sisters lived next door. Down the street Kitty's parents moved in. His own family grew quickly. His first child, Lloyd, was born in 1890 and was soon followed by John (1892), Catherine (1894), David (1895), Frances (1898), and Robert (1903).

"Most of our friends (some of ourselves) are, when it comes to Architecture, Art, and Decoration, masquerading in borrowed finery: borrowed of another epoch that cannot honestly fit them."

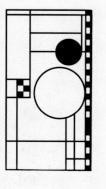

Above the mantel Wright inscribed in an oak panel his new motto, "Truth Is life." The old battle between Truth and the rest of the world seemed to have been resolved—at least for a while.

Life in Oak Park was not without its problems. Frank Lloyd Wright battled all his life against the thinking that constrained other people's lives. Money was just one of those ideas that, as Wright saw it, impeded human progress. When he wished to build an addition to the house or buy some artwork, he would not let the bank's trivial point that he had no money in his account stop him. Even when checks were returned marked "NSF"(Non-Sufficient Funds) and accompanied by a stern note of warning, Wright would not be discouraged. "There'll be more, somewhere," he would cheerfully say.

The sheriff was a familiar figure in the house; upon occasion he stayed all night, waiting for payment on an outstanding debt. At least once, Wright woke up in the morning, deeply in debt and harassed by creditors, and went out, sold a valuable piece of art, paid off what he owed, and continued on a buying spree that ended with him even deeper in debt, but very contented, at the end of the day.

Despite its occasional difficulties, life in Oak Park seemed, at least to the Wright children, a long round of picnics and parties. A large addition was built for a playroom that was almost as big as all of the rest of the house. There was room for roughhousing, learning lessons, practicing music, and giving amateur dramatic performances. There Kitty governed over neighborhood kindergarten classes and the children held concerts, each playing his own instrument. On Sundays the family would worship together with Uncle Jenkin at All Souls Church.

Frank Lloyd Wright during this time had become virtually indispensable to Adler & Sullivan. Now in charge of a squad of thirty draftsmen, he was involved in some of the firm's most important and influential projects, including the Auditorium Building on Michigan Avenue in Chicago and the Transportation Building at the Chicago World's Fair. The majority of the projects handled by Adler & Sullivan were downtown commercial buildings—theaters, warehouses, hotels, and office buildings. Occasionally they would be asked to design a residence, but this was only an inconvenience to the large firm. For special clients, however, exceptions were made, and Wright was assigned this work. Sullivan's friend James Charnley was one person who could not be put off. The house built for him in downtown Chicago shows the union of Sullivan's and Wright's architectural ideas. Its stark simplicity of massing and interior complexity gives an indication of Wright's early promise.

Word of Wright's talents soon spread throughout the small but growing population of Chicago's suburban professionals. Before long Wright was designing houses on his own in the evenings, while working for Adler & Sullivan during the day. But this was a breach of contract, and eventually word reached Sullivan, who expected Wright to spend all his energies on the firm's contracts. Wright was at the drafting board in his office when Sullivan came in to confront him. Sullivan turned his withering scorn on Wright and ordered him to stop work on these "bootleg houses." Wright, as inflexible as his mentor, refused. He threw his pencil down on the table and walked out.

Once again, Wright was on his own. He had abandoned the comfortable security of a steady income with one of Chicago's most prestigious architectural firms for the uncertainties of working for himself. As it happened, it marked an important turning point in Louis Sullivan's life as well as in Wright's.

Wright and Sullivan had shared much in common, most important, perhaps, a radical sense of the possibilities of a new American architecture. In both cases their vision of the future was coupled with an indomitable, even arrogant, faith in their own abilities to bring it to reality. But the courses of their careers took drastically different paths after Wright left Sullivan's office.

Sullivan's ideas for this new American architecture perhaps reached their fulfillment in the Transportation building he designed for the Chicago World's Fair in 1893, the same year Wright left the firm. With its gigantic

polychromed arch, however, the building seemed markedly out of place. Sullivan alone had refused to comply with the decision that all of the fair's buildings conform to a single style. With Sullivan's stunning exception, the fair was a great exhibition of classical architecture, imported from Ancient Rome by way of the Ecole des Beaux-Arts in Paris. Buildings with sparkling white plaster columns, domes, and arches, in imitation of marble, stood erect like soldiers at attention on the parade ground. This was the death knell for an American architecture, although perhaps only Louis Sullivan heard it at the time. For the next half century, American architecture would find inspiration not on its own soil but in the ancient capitals of Europe.

As it happened, the partnership of Adler & Sullivan fell apart within two years of Wright's departure. Sullivan, without his right-hand man, alienated from his workers and abandoned by his partner, was soon

THE WILLIAM H. WINSLOW HOUSE IN RIVER FOREST, ILLINOIS, 1893. THIS DRAWING SHOWS THE BUILDING IN PERSPECTIVE, ITS PLAN (BOTTOM LEFT), AND DECORATIVE DETAILS OF THE FRONT WINDOW AND PLANTERS (RIGHT).

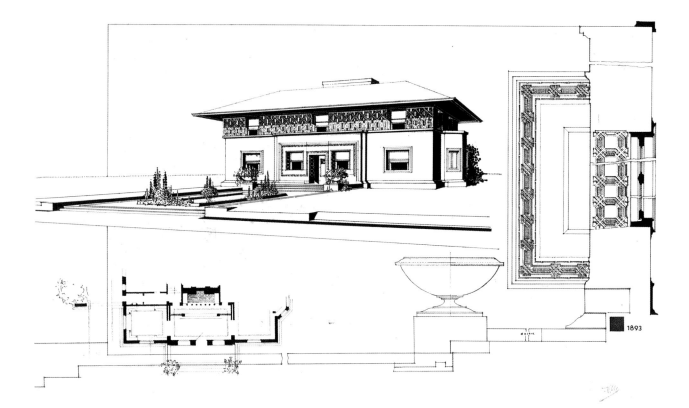

1893

deserted by his clients as well. During the economic depression that dogged the middle of the 1890s, few clients wanted to gamble with the erratic genius. In the final decades of his life he continued to build some extraordinary buildings, but with much smaller budgets than he had been accustomed to and in out-of-the-way places. His continued fame today rests chiefly upon his writings, especially his *Autobiography of an Idea*, and upon the progress of his most famous student and admirer, Frank

THE WILLIAM H. WINSLOW HOUSE'S UNUSUAL LOW ROOF STRETCHING OUT BEYOND THE WALLS WAS CRITICIZED AT THE TIME.

41

Lloyd Wright. Increasingly morose, unable to pay the rent for either his office or the cheap hotel where he lived, possibly alcoholic as well, Louis Sullivan died in 1924.

After a shaky start, Frank Lloyd Wright's course over the next few years took a much more auspicious path. The first house he built after leaving Sullivan was for Wright's friend, William Winslow. Some people thought it should have been his last. Its severe rectilinear geometry, with a huge low roof stretching out beyond the walls, made it the butt of many jokes in the neighborhood. Some even said that Mr. Winslow had to sneak down back alleys to his morning train in order to avoid being laughed at. The characteristics that made the house unusual, perhaps even awkward-looking, however, are exactly the same features that Wright would refine and shape over the next few years to create the most dynamic and beautiful houses ever built in America.

Wright's architectural experiments, despite their critics, soon found a growing number of admirers. One evening, shortly after he left Adler and Sullivan, Frank and Kitty were invited to a dinner party at a neighbor's house. The guests included Daniel Burnham, whose firm of Burnham & Root was one of Adler & Sullivan's leading rivals. Burnham had been the architect responsible for the decision to use classical design at the Chicago World's Fair. He was very enthusiastic about Wright's work and had arranged this meeting specifically for the purpose of making him an offer. After dinner Wright, Burnham, and their host adjourned to the study, and Burnham made Wright a proposal few men could have resisted. Burnham would send Wright to Paris to study at the Ecole des Beaux-Arts, with all expenses paid. When Wright returned he would have a job with Burnham, perhaps a partnership. Wright, hearing this, sat down, embarrassed, not knowing what to say.

Burnham saw Wright hesitate.

"Another year, and it will be too late, Frank."

"It's too late now, I'm afraid," Wright finally replied. He had been too long with Sullivan, he said, too influenced by Sullivan's feelings toward classicism, to be able to accept.

It was a historic meeting between one of America's greatest exponents of classicism and one of its greatest critics. Burnham was astonished. How could anyone reject this certain ticket to success? He argued that Greek and Roman architecture was the purest, the most beautiful in the world. Its classic lines and perfect proportions were the basis of all good building. Wright, more embarrassed than argumentative, respond-

*THE UNITY TEMPLE,
OAK PARK,
ILLINOIS, 1904.
FRANK LLOYD
WRIGHT BUILT A
CHURCH WITHOUT A
STEEPLE, SAYING
"RELIGION AND ART
ARE FORMS OF INNER
EXPERIENCE."*

ed no, he didn't think so. Classicism and the beaux-arts just seemed like a jail to him. Wright's friend and host interrupted, "Frank, don't you realize what this offer means to you? . . . Think of your future, think of your family." Still, Wright would not be dissuaded. The three men left the study. Wright helped Kitty on with her things and the couple went home. He did not mention to her what had happened until long afterward.

Wright's self-confidence was soon rewarded. Over the next decade and a half, he helped to create an architectural style that totally transformed the way most Americans lived. It became known as the Prairie style, and it was almost solely the invention of Frank Lloyd Wright. Only he would not have called it a style. Styles of architecture, to Wright, were merely passing fads, the whims of theorists driven by commercial rather than artistic concerns. The architecture of the Prairie school was more than a style of architecture; to Frank Lloyd Wright, it was a philosophy of life.

Over the next few years, Wright would design a series of houses in Oak Park and neighboring communities that would revolutionize

"A house,
we like
to believe,
is *in status
quo* a noble
consort
to man and
the trees;
therefore
the house
should have
repose and
such texture
as will quiet
the whole and
make it
graciously
at one with
external
nature."

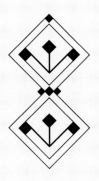

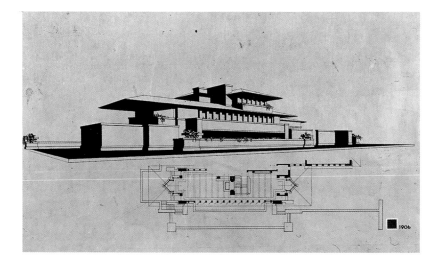

LEFT: *PHOTO AND
PLAN OF THE
FREDERICK C. ROBIE
HOUSE, CHICAGO,
ILLINOIS, 1906.*

American architecture. In houses Wright built for Ward Willits (1901), Frank Thomas (1901), Susan Lawrence Dana (1902), Arthur Heurtley (1902), Edwin H. Cheney (1903), Frederick Robie (1906), Avery Coonley (1907), and a dozen others, Wright developed his philosophy of organic architecture. Its central tenet was that a house should be truthful to its purpose, its site, and its materials. Wright sought in all of his buildings an ideal harmony between the natural environment, the materials of construction, the purpose of the structure, and the personality of its occupants. The Prairie House was meant to look as though it had grown naturally out of the soil, with horizontal lines and earth tones blending into its surroundings. In a time when houses were generally designed to pierce the sky with pointed gables and many chimneys, when wood was painted and brick plastered, Wright's designs were apt

"I had an idea that the planes parallel to earth in buildings identify themselves with the ground—make the building belong to the ground. At any rate I perceived it and put it to work. I had an idea that every house in that low region should begin _on_ the ground— not _in_ it, as they then began, with damp cellars. This idea put the house up on the 'prairie basement' I devised, entirely above the ground. And an idea that the house should _look_ as though it began there _at_ the ground put a projecting base-course as a visible edge to this foundation, where, as a platform, it was seen as evident preparation for

to startle their early viewers despite the buildings' seemingly unassuming intentions.

Wright brought some of the new technology that had revolutionized city building into his suburban houses. Steel and glass allowed Wright to completely destroy the idea that a house was only a box to live in. Realizing that a roof was best supported not at its edges or corners but closer to its center, Wright began his experiments in cantilevered construction. He always imagined that a house should be more like a tree growing out from its center, rather than merely being the sum of its exterior walls. This was a radically new conception of building, one in which the space within was more important than the containing forms without. This mental breakthrough allowed Wright to physically break through the material boundaries that separated the occupants of a building from the natural environment. Spaces became much more complex. They could no longer be imagined in the terms of plane geometry, bounded by lines and angles. Centers of activity flowed from area to area, from outside to inside.

The lack of rigid boundaries opened up a sense of extraordinary possibilities, a physical freedom that Wright never tired of comparing to America's political freedoms. The house on the prairie was an expression of an architecture of democracy. Of course, Wright's idea of democracy was perhaps not the same as everyone else's. As he described it, democracy was the highest form of aristocracy. Not everyone was ready for this democracy; only those who were willing to commit themselves to its ideals and to take the risks that that entailed were apt to be members of Wright's democratic community.

As much as Wright was opposed to formulas, certain features were common to almost all of his Prairie houses. The most important element was a massive central chimney, which was the spiritual center of the home. Its heat and light were symbolic of the warmth and radiance of the family itself. The route to the hearth was a psychological as well as physical passage. The visitor entered the house from the street through an unobtrusive doorway that was sometimes difficult to find. Wright rarely built a grand entranceway. Inside, the visitor often passed from dimly illuminated spaces to brilliantly lit areas, from low, narrow spaces to broad, open areas. Progress through the house was not meant to follow the routes of logic. The spatial complexity mirrored the psychological complexity of its unique human inhabitants. Wright often praised the Gothic architecture of medieval churches for many of the qualities that he gloried in his own work. Both shared a reverence for spatial and emotional complexity, and a rejection of classical formalism. But Wright was never comfortable with the striving for great heights typical of Gothic architecture. His Prairie houses were not meant to be castles in the air or fingers pointing to heaven. They were completely of this earth. That was the whole point. They grew naturally from, and never left, the soil. They were a celebration of a perfect harmony of man's psyche and the natural world that he inhabited. The Prairie House, like most of Wright's later architecture, emphasized its horizontality. The pitch of his roofs over time became lower and lower and, ultimately, flat.

The houses ideally suited the new life-styles of suburbanites. Outside of the crowded cities, there was more land on which to spread out. The compact buildings of the city frequently contained several families on different levels and housed servants or tenants in their damp basements or hot attics. The Prairie House had no attic or basement. Only one social class lived in the suburbs. Servants and other laborers generally rode into the city in the morning by streetcar and left their jobs at night. The middle-class family was increasingly a refuge from the harsh realities of the larger world. Isolated, removed from the city and from people they often could no longer understand, they were able to imagine a world of ideal harmony between themselves and nature.

Many of these houses were designed in the studio Wright now built adjacent to his house in Oak Park. At last he was able to join home and work in one, for the most part, unified whole. It was not always a perfect union. His children soon found passageways to the balcony overlooking the large space set aside for draftsmen, and they would sometimes throw down scraps of paper and run off giggling as the employees looked up to see where the rain of paper was coming from. Perhaps Wright's moving all his work into his home also put a strain on his relationship with Kitty. Increasingly, his work subordinated all areas of his life and home.

A large willow grew on the lot and as Wright enlarged the house to build his studio, instead of cutting the tree down, he designed a corridor around it between the house and studio. Visitors constantly remarked on how odd it was to have a tree growing out of a house. But Wright realized that the tree was an essential part of his home. Nature and his life would have to find a harmony. Perhaps Wright looked at that tree, poking through the roof of his house, and imagined that he too might escape into the light and the open air above.

"Nature is a good teacher. I am a child of hers, and apart from her precepts, cannot flourish. I cannot work as well as she, perhaps, but at least can shape my work to sympathize with what seems beautiful to me in hers."

CHAPTER FOUR

MAMAH CHENEY

Frank Lloyd Wright had become very successful by inventing houses for new suburbanites, but he himself was increasingly uncomfortable trying to pretend that he was one of those people. As Wright later wrote, "I had almost reached my fortieth year: Weary, I was losing grip on my work and even interest in it." He felt that he was "up against a dead wall. I could see no way out. Because I did not know what I wanted, I wanted to go away." And so he left.

The occasion for his abandoning his home and business in Chicago in 1909 was an offer by the German publishing firm of Ernst Wasmuth to print an edition of plans, illustrations, and photographs of his architecture. This project would require Wright's constant attention as the plates were engraved and printed, and would necessitate a long trip to Germany. That Wright decided to make the trip not with his wife but with the wife

OVERLEAF: THE INTERIOR OF THE C. THAXTER SHAW HOUSE, MONTREAL, CANADA, 1906.

MR. C. THAXTER SHAW
RESIDENCE ▲ MONTRE
DINING ROOM
FRANK LLOYD WRIGHT
ARCHITECT
OAK PARK ▲ ILLINOIS

of a client, Mamah Borthwick Cheney, insured that the newspaper press-es in America would be every bit as active as those in Germany.

Mamah (pronounced "May-mah") Cheney was what a later genera-tion would call a free spirit. Although she was described by some as "capricious and temperamental," she was also deeply interested in the arts and literature. A university graduate and a librarian before she mar-ried, she became interested in French and German literature, especially Goethe, and, with Wright, would publish translations of the works of the early Swedish feminist Ellen Key. Wright and Mrs. Cheney had become acquainted while he was designing a house for her and her husband in Oak Park. Before long their affair was a serious one and they each asked their spouses for a divorce. When their requests were denied, they simply took off together.

This event became one of the great scandals that interrupted the seemingly even flow of Wright's career as an architect. The crisis broke when an enterprising reporter for the *Chicago Tribune* found out that Wright and Mrs. Cheney had signed into a Berlin hotel as "husband and wife." The *Tribune* then published a lengthy interview with the confused and dejected Catherine, who insisted that Wright would yet come to his senses and return to her.

Newspaper reporters ultimately cornered Wright. In a series of inter-views Wright defended abandoning his family in the name of a "higher law." His behavior was inspired by love and his regard for honesty. His actions were, he implied, the justifiable acts of a creative and divinely inspired genius. In addition, he criticized traditional concepts of marriage as a form of property and equated it with slavery.

The newspapers jumped on these pronouncements, describing both Wright and Mrs. Cheney as insane and immoral. The press—in this, the golden age of "yellow journalism" and muckraking—was increasingly skilled in feeding a new reading public's hunger for sensationalism. In the process, the papers succeeded in turning the private domestic problems of two couples into a cause célèbre. Wright, during the course of his life, would slowly learn how to turn the public's appetite for the dramatic to his own advantage, but this was still in the future.

The newspapers, for their part, despite their equivocal motives, had succeeded in uncovering—and perhaps, to some extent, in manufactur-ing—one of the central themes in the life of Frank Lloyd Wright. As much as Wright strived to accomplish a harmonious balance between his archi-tecture and its natural environment—a unity of all its various parts—

Wright, for most of his life, was unable to find a similar balance between his own creative individuality and the larger community he inhabited. This problem was not unique to Wright. Since the time of the ancient Greeks, such overwhelming pride had been condemned as hubris, the fatal flaw that inevitably brought down the wrath of the gods. From the antinomian controversy of Anne Hutchinson in Colonial New England to the philosophy of civil disobedience as proposed by Henry David Thoreau, American history has been bedeviled by the question: Should an individual follow his or her own truths, or those of the society to which he or she belongs? The question is unlikely ever to have a definitive answer. But for Frank Lloyd Wright, as for the many others who were confronted by this issue, the truth was that, as you sow, so shall you reap. For years to come Frank Lloyd Wright would harvest the effects, for good and for ill, of his decision.

Wright had once again run away from a secure and comfortable world to one full of uncertainties. In leaving Chicago and Oak Park he had entered a far larger stage. Over the years he would become the best-known and most influential architect in the world, and the publication of his work in Germany was the first step in that direction. European architects, whose work would both spread Wright's philosophy of building and compete with his for popular acclaim, got some of their first glimpses of the promise of modern architecture by studying the portfolios of Wright's work published by Ernst Wasmuth in 1910.

European architects were most impressed, however, not with Wright's domestic architecture and its philosophy of organic design, but with two public buildings he had designed during his Oak Park years. One of these was the Larkin Building in Buffalo, New York—Wright's first large-scale experiment, as he described it, in "breaking the box." Public buildings, even more than private homes, Wright realized, were apt to be merely boxes inside of boxes. The people who worked or lived in them had a tendency to be seen merely as the contents of their rigid containers. The modern office building thus had a powerful tendency to dehumanize its inhabitants, Wright believed, just as modern commercial practices dehumanized the larger society. By simply moving the stair towers of the Larkin Building free of the central block, Wright was successful in creating a dramatic building mass reminiscent of the architecture of ancient Egypt. Inside a vast central court, secretaries worked on the ground floor, while the company's managers occupied open offices located nearby. On the balconies above specialized tasks were performed. Wright liked

OPPOSITE: *THE LARKIN COMPANY ADMINISTRATION BUILDING IN BUFFALO, NEW YORK, 1906.*

LEFT: *THE ATRIUM OF THE LARKIN BUILDING, WHERE "THE LARKIN FAMILY," AS THE WORKERS WERE CALLED, FILLED OUT MAIL ORDERS UNDER THE SUPERVISION OF THEIR MANAGERS.*

ABOVE AND OPPOSITE:
"LA MINIATURA," A HOUSE
DESIGNED AND BUILT FOR
MRS. ALICE MILLARD IN
PASADENA, CALIFORNIA,
1923. IT WAS FRANK LLOYD
WRIGHT'S FIRST CONCRETE-
BLOCK HOUSE.

to think that the effect of the open plan was to create a space for what he called a "great official family at work."

The other major building that had a dramatic influence on young European architects was the church for the small community of Unitarians in Oak Park. Throughout his life Wright usually created his best architecture when he had an unlimited budget—or a severely limited one. Few commissions tested his abilities to design on a shoestring more than Unity Church. The congregation of about four hundred could afford only

RIGHT: *THE ROMEO AND JULIET WINDMILL TOWER BUILT FOR THE HILLSIDE HOME SCHOOL, 1896. THE DIAMOND-SHAPED PORTION, ROMEO, PROVIDES STABILITY AND DEFLECTS THE STRONG WINDS FROM THE SOUTHWEST.*

OPPOSITE: *TALIESIN, FRANK LLOYD WRIGHT'S HOME IN SPRING GREEN, WISCONSIN.*

$45,000 to build a structure to house both their religious services and social activities. Wright resolved the problem of constructing the most building for the least money by turning to concrete, one of the oldest and, at that time, least appreciated building materials in the history of architecture. Concrete—essentially, sand, gravel, and lime—was cheap

"Go to Nature, thou builder of houses, consider her ways and do not be petty and foolish. Let your home appear to grow easily from its site and shape it to sympathize with the sur-roundings if Nature is manifest there, and if not, try and be as quiet, substantial, and organic as she would have been if she had the chance."

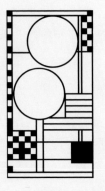

enough, but the real expenses were the wood forms needed to hold the concrete in place while it hardened. Wright's accomplishment was a design that used a minimum number of wooden forms, which could be dismantled and reused in different parts of the building. The result was a structure of simple but powerful massing that reflected a perfect unity between the nature of the material and the needs of the congregation.

When Wright returned to the United States with Mamah Cheney, he began to build his second home. Wright sometimes told the story of the holy man who, yearning to see God, climbed up the highest mountain. When he reached the summit he heard a voice call to him, "Get down...go back." The seeker was told to "go down into the valley below where his own people were—there only could he look upon God's coun-tenance." This was the very advice he took now as he returned to Spring Green, Wisconsin, and began to build a house on the hillside where he had played as a boy.

He called the place Taliesin, after an ancient Welsh poet who cele-brated the art and culture of Wales. In English the word means "shining brow," and Wright thought that was an appropriate image for the house he built not on the hill but, as he said, "of the hill." Like all of the homes he designed for himself, it was a structure that would grow in fits and starts, mirroring the erratic course of Wright's own life. Built of the local yellow sand-limestone, the low one-story house wrapping around the earth appeared to be a natural outcropping. Its walls and pavements merged into the hillside so subtly that it was difficult to point to the spot where the hill ended and the house began. Nearby stood the farms and houses of his uncles, and his aunts' Hillside Home School. Overlooking it all was the odd-looking windmill Wright had designed to pull water out of underground springs to feed the school. Interlocking columns, one octagonal and one diamond-shaped, provided extraordinary stability and led Wright to name the windmill Romeo and Juliet. It was the cause of great controversy among the Lloyd-Joneses when it was first built, and long after seemed to signify to Wright his new status as a leading mem-ber in the family.

Wright's goal now was to build not just a new house for himself and Mamah Cheney but also a new life. Taliesin was designed as the center-piece of a self-sufficient estate, where Wright imagined he could join his architectural practice with farming. He would raise cattle and sheep in the fields surrounding Taliesin and grow fruits and vegetables in its gar-dens. Wright's return to nature, however, was not a rejection of modern civilization. He knew that his new role of architect/gentleman farmer existed only because the automobile and the telephone had made such an arrangement possible.

Despite Wright's plans and accomplishments in this period he still was not satisfied; perhaps he never would be. He had felt, he said, uncomfortable in the role of a father, yet now on visits to Chicago he would sometimes drive to Oak Park at night. Gazing out of his car window, he saw the lights streaming from the open windows of his home. He heard the murmured voices of his children as they called to each other. He listened to the music coming from the piano and heard singing, and then he would drive away. Over the years he would learn how to forget.

Wright's major project during these years was the vast entertainment park named Midway Gardens, which covered an entire city block in south Chicago. It was designed as a cultural center in which an elite clientele could hear a concert while others could drink, dine, and dance in an outdoor garden setting. Unfortunately, it was constantly beset by financial problems and following the passage of Prohibition in 1919, it quickly passed into bankruptcy. It survives now only in plans, illustrations, and photographs that document its extraordinary, fantasy-like qualities. When it was razed in 1929, Wright took delight in the fact that it was so massive and so solidly built that the wrecking contractor was forced into bankruptcy.

In 1914 Wright's life suddenly took a dramatic and tragic turn. He was working at the small office he had built at Midway Gardens while it was under construction. While he was eating his lunch, a stenographer from the Garden's front office walked in. "Mr. Wright, you're wanted on the telephone," she said.

He went out to take the call and then returned to the office. His face was white, and everyone in the room turned silent. Wright clung to the table for support and groaned. "Taliesin is on fire," he finally announced.

Wright soon learned the rest of the story. Mamah Cheney and six others had died at the hands of a crazed servant, who had set the building afire and then killed the fleeing inhabitants with an axe as they passed through the doors. Something died in Wright at the same time. It was as though the flames that had taken his home and his love had also destroyed a part of Wright. His youth, his overpowering optimism, now lay behind him as he was forced to set out once again into an uncertain future.

"The Imperial Hotel
 is designed as a
 system of gardens
 and sunken
 gardens and
 terraced gardens—
 of balconies that
 are gardens and
 loggias that are
 also gardens—and
 roofs that are
 gardens—until
 the whole arrange-
 ment becomes an
 interpenetration of
 gardens. Japan is
 Garden-land."

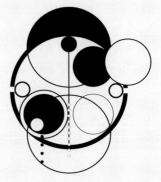

CHAPTER FIVE

A LONG WINTER

Frank Lloyd Wright is often said to have had two careers. The one which began in Chicago and Oak Park was now ended. His second career still lay several years in the future. For the next two decades Frank Lloyd Wright completed relatively few building projects. The several houses he designed between 1914 and about 1930 are best known for Wright's intriguing experiments in materials and forms, but they have rarely been as highly praised by architectural historians as were his earliest and latest work. The great exception to this was Wright's stunning success in designing the Imperial Hotel in Tokyo.

Wright had long been fascinated by Japan and its unique sense of aesthetics. He had perhaps first seen an example of Japanese building at the Chicago World's Fair in 1893. In 1905 he made his first visit to Japan with his wife, Catherine, and began his collection of Japanese

ABOVE AND OPPOSITE:
EXTERIOR AND INTERIOR
VIEWS OF THE IMPERIAL
HOTEL, BUILT IN TOKYO,
JAPAN, 1916.

artwork. Soon Wright became a serious collector of Oriental art. He was especially interested in Japanese woodblock prints, which seemed to him to distill the complexities of nature down to their simplest forms. By 1912 Wright wrote his first book, not on architecture, but on the art of the Japanese print. This interest in Japan and her culture had to be a plus when he came to the attention of highly placed individuals in Japanese business and government. The island nation was just

OPPOSITE: A COLORED-PEN-CIL DRAWING OF THE GORDON STRONG PLANETARIUM PROJECT, SUGAR LOAF MOUNTAIN, MARYLAND, 1924.

beginning her entrance upon the world stage, and as European and American entrepreneurs flocked to her shores at the beginning of the century, it soon became apparent that these new visitors needed suitable accommodations.

Traditional Japanese architecture evolved over the centuries, and although it contained elements of the Chinese style, it was unaffected by Western ideas of style and comfort. Buildings with tile roofs were constructed on sturdy wooden supports, and interiors had sliding screens with paper panels to vary the room configurations and meet the changing needs of the household. Woven floor mats (tatami) created a standardized scale that determined the size and shapes of rooms and the placement of partitions. Large overhanging eaves and porches allowed a gradual transition from the outside environment to the interior of the house. In addition, the Japanese lived at floor level. The traditional Japanese house had no sofas or chairs. Individuals kneeled, or sat on pillows. Beds were laid out at night and stored away during the day. Wright, like many other visitors to Japan, marveled over the simplicity, efficiency, cleanliness, and spiritual significance inherent in the Japanese home. But such buildings required a transformation of habits, and ways of thinking, that foreign businessmen were not always eager to make.

The Japanese Imperial Household agreed to share the costs with some of the country's leading industrialists for a new hotel in Tokyo to meet the needs of foreign visitors, and they selected Wright to be its architect. It was Wright's job to create a marriage between Eastern and Western building practices and designs. Probably no one else in the world at that time was more capable of accomplishing such a task. Wright had already been greatly inspired by many of the principles of traditional Japanese aesthetics, and the Prairie House itself shared much in common with the traditional Japanese home.

Wright spent eight years (1914–1922) designing and overseeing the construction of the Imperial Hotel, living for much of that time in Japan. Not only did he have to find a harmony between Eastern and Western design concepts, he had to bridge the gulf between different social customs and business practices. Laborers who lived with their families in the building while it was under construction, and who sometimes refused to work in the strange and often impractical ways they were directed, frequently disrupted work until accommodations were finally made between all the parties involved. Certainly Wright's unbending personality drove the work forward in Japan, just as it often did in America. Wright even

designed silverware, plates, cups, saucers, drinking glasses, carpets, murals, wastepaper baskets, and cuspidors.

The greatest problem Wright faced in designing the Imperial Hotel, however, was the threat of an earthquake. Even as Wright was working in his Tokyo office one day, just before noon, a gigantic jolt lifted the whole building, sending all of Wright's draftsmen—and their drawing boards—sprawling to the floor. Draftsmen and workmen hurried from the site, throwing down their tools and running for their lives. Wright was knocked down by the rushing crowd, and as he lay on the ground he saw the land swell as a wave formed and passed by. He heard the collapse of chimneys and the hideous crushing and grinding noises as buildings heaved and groaned.

Wright early on had recognized the nature of the problem and its solution. Instead of fighting an earthquake, his idea was to build a structure that, as he said, would "sympathize with it and outwit it." His building would float like a ship on the unstable earth below. He took borings in the earth and made tests at the site, and found that under an eight-foot layer of surface soil lay a strata of mud from sixty to seventy feet deep. The foundations of the Imperial Hotel were built to ride upon this deposit of mud, and the building was constructed in flexible sections that would expand and contract with a passing tremor.

The Imperial Hotel was a stunning achievement both technologically and visually. The building delighted its many visitors from its opening in 1923 until it was finally torn down in 1968 when its site in downtown Tokyo ultimately proved too valuable to be used for the low, sprawling hotel.

Shortly after Wright completed his work, his experiment in earthquake-proof building was tested. He read the news first in the papers: All of Tokyo, including the Imperial Hotel, they announced, had been destroyed in the most terrible earthquake in its history. Ten days later Wright received a more accurate report. A telegram from Tokyo reached him stating, "HOTEL STANDS UNDAMAGED AS MONUMENT OF YOUR GENIUS HUNDREDS OF HOMELESS PROVIDED BY PERFECTLY MAINTAINED SERVICE CONGRATULATIONS."

This was perhaps the single brightest light in Frank Lloyd Wright's professional life during the 1920s. The Taliesin fire had been the beginning of a long emotional descent that Wright was only gradually able to reverse. Wright for much of this time was still healing his wounds from the tragedy of 1914. After the fire and the death of Mamah Cheney, he received hundreds of expressions of sympathy from friends and from strangers. One day, in an effort to put the anguish behind him, he tied up these letters, still unread, in a bundle and set them on fire.

One letter, however, he did not burn. It was from a woman who had herself known tragedy and who offered Wright some solace. After a short correspondence they met. Her name was Miriam Noel, a woman driven from Paris during the First World War. She seemed to Wright brilliant and sophisticated, and shortly after Catherine finally granted Wright a divorce in 1922, Wright and Miriam Noel were married.

Wright would later describe his situation with an old aphorism: "Drowning men clutch at straws." It was an unhappy affair apparently from the start. The couple lived together only five months before disagreements and jealousies forced them to separate. Wright's marriage to Miriam Noel lasted only four years (1923–1927), but they were among the most turbulent years in a lifetime of tumults and uproars.

He now began to rebuild Taliesin, but twice it caught fire, and he had to start over again. Miriam, emotionally unstable when she met Wright, grew increasingly troubled. In 1924 Frank Lloyd Wright finally met the woman who would ultimately bring as much peace and serenity to his life as he would ever know, but the immediate result was to throw Miriam Noel over the edge into the depths of outrage, jealousy, and despair. She became a maelstrom of emotions that Wright, unlike the Imperial Hotel, was unable simply to float over.

The focus of Miriam's troubles and the source of Wright's tranquility was Olga Ivanovna Milanoff Hinzenburg. They met in 1924 in Chicago at a matinee performance of a Russian ballet company. He was 57; she, 26. Despite the disparity in their ages and the fact that both were married at the time, their relationship blossomed. Their strengths and weaknesses so complemented each other that together they would grow and develop in ways they could not have individually. Olgivanna, as she was called, would have such a strong influence on the course of the remainder of Wright's life that it is difficult to imagine that his later successes could have happened without her. Shortly after their meeting she and her seven-year-old daughter, Svetlana, were living with him at Taliesin, and before 1925 was over Olgivanna and Wright had a daughter, whom they named Iovanna.

As happy as these events were, they were only a prologue to the turbulent drama that followed in 1926, one of the most tumultuous years of Wright's life. The events were set in motion by Miriam's refusal to grant

FRANK LLOYD
WRIGHT, 1928.

Wright a divorce and her pressing a legal action against Olgivanna for "alienation of affections." Wright's lawyer suggested that Wright and his new family disappear for a period of time, waiting, in effect, for things to "blow over." As well-meaning as the advice was, Wright's disappearance created a flurry of speculation in the newspapers about the scandalous architect and his affairs. New charges were now pressed by Olgivanna's ex-husband, despite the fact that the couple had by this time been properly divorced. He charged Wright with abducting his daughter, Svetlana, sued him for a quarter-million dollars for "alienation of affections," and offered a five-hundred dollar reward for his arrest. The fact that Wright, Olgivanna, Svetlana, and Iovanna had crossed state lines in the course of their flight from justice, brought federal charges as well. Now even immigration officials took an interest, charging that Olgivanna had broken the terms of her legal status as a "resident alien." Trouble mounted upon trouble as lawyers, newspapermen, and politicians saw their opportunities to make money, grab headlines, and gain notoriety, all at the expense of Wright and Olgivanna.

The culmination of these events occurred on October 20, 1926, when a horde of newspaper reporters, photographers, sheriffs, and lawyers appeared at the cottage in Minnesota where the small family was in hiding. Wright was marched off as camera shutters clicked and

flashbulbs exploded. At the Minneapolis jail, Wright was led to a small cell and experienced the sensations common perhaps to every incarcerated individual. He heard the heavy metal doors open and slam shut as he entered, and he fought off the feeling of suffocation as he stared at the soiled mattress on one side of his six-by-six-foot cell and at the dirty water closet nearby.

Wright was arraigned the following morning and returned to jail for a second night before his lawyers were finally able to arrange his

HOLLYHOCK HOUSE, BUILT FOR ALINE BARNSDALL IN LOS ANGELES, CALIFORNIA, 1917.

HOLLYHOCK HOUSE, BUILT FOR ALINE BARNSDALL IN LOS ANGELES, CALIFORNIA, 1917.

release. Every citizen, guilty of a crime or not, Wright later argued, should, as a part of his education, spend two nights in such a jail, if they would truly understand the nature of the society to which they belonged.

Wright was barely out of jail, and the slow process of trying to clear his name had not yet begun, when financial problems were added to his legal troubles. Wright's business had been in decline in the aftermath of his long absence in Japan, and the continuing note of scandal attached to his name scared off many lucrative commissions. In addition, the large expenses of rebuilding his fire-ravaged home were adding up. Finally, the bank that held Wright's mortgage on Taliesin foreclosed when Wright was unable to make payments.

Wright was forced to leave Taliesin, and the bank began to auction off his furniture, equipment, livestock, and art collection. Wright was saved from destitution only when a group of his friends, family, and clients joined together to help him through his difficulties. They hired lawyers to clear Wright of the greatly exaggerated charges against him and formed "Frank Lloyd Wright, Incorporated," gambling that Wright's future work would enable the architect to satisfy the calls of his creditors and repay

their purchase of shares. It would be a long time, however, before their confidence was rewarded. In the meantime, Wright's life and work was to be the legal property of others.

Wright was finally able to secure a divorce from Miriam in 1927, when her lawyers, witnessing her tailspin into irrationality, finally deserted her. The final coda to their relationship occurred when Miriam broke into the house Wright and Olgivanna were renting in La Jolla, California, while they tried to regain possession of Taliesin. Finding no one home, Miriam went on a rampage, smashing costly furniture and taking the items she did not destroy. A few years later Miriam Noel Wright died in a sanitarium after suffering from, as it was officially described, "exhaustion following delirium."

On August 25, 1928, Wright and Olgivanna were finally married, and took their first steps on the long road out of the depths of their financial and legal problems. Unfortunately, their journey had just begun when the nation took a different path. On "Black Tuesday," October 29, 1929, the Wall Street stock-market crash triggered the Great Depression that afflicted the nation for over a decade. Bank closings, business failures, and unemployment swept the country.

RIGHT: *THE COURTYARD OF HOLLYHOCK HOUSE, WITH ITS POND AND STREAM.*

OPPOSITE: *A RUG DESIGN BY FRANK LLOYD WRIGHT FOR THE MAX HOFFMAN RESIDENCE IN RYE, NEW YORK, 1957.*

It is perhaps the mark of great people that they are able turn their lives from misfortune to triumph, to find strength in tragedy, and to create good out of evil. Frank Lloyd Wright had ample opportunity to hone this skill. It was not a task, however, that even he could perform overnight. Throughout the period from the first fire at Taliesin until the 1930s, Wright continued to experiment in new architectural forms. His construction of Hollyhock house for Aline Barnsdall in Los Angeles, and his experiments in concrete-block construction were radical departures from his older Prairie style work and important influences upon his later architecture, but these buildings are now regarded more for their drama than their practicality.

The years to follow saw Wright complete fewer and fewer commissions as he turned his energies increasingly toward writing and lecturing. His autobiography, which was begun while he and Olgivanna were in hiding, is a monument to his life and his philosophy of architecture, and would eventually have a dramatic influence upon a younger generation of architects. It is still the best source of information on Wright. By the time it was finally published in 1932, however, most serious architectural critics recognized the aging Wright as a grand old man in American architecture, but one whose influence and accomplishments were all in the past.

BOOK CASE

BOOK

"Nothing is more
difficult to achieve than
the integral simplicity
of organic nature amid
the tangled confusions
of the innumerable
relics of form that
encumber life for us.
To achieve it in any
degree means a serious
devotion to the 'under-
neath' in an attempt to
grasp the *nature* of
building a beautiful
building beautifully,
as organically true in
itself, to itself and to
its purpose, as any
tree or flower."

CHAPTER SIX

REGENERATION

Far from ready to be put out to pasture, Frank Lloyd Wright was now just beginning the most creative phase of his life's work. Probably the most important step Wright took in rejuvenating his declining career as an architect was the establishment of the Taliesin Fellowship. In 1932 Wright sent a small group of friends a notice announcing that he would accept apprentices to reside and work with him at Taliesin.

It was a brilliant stroke. At $650 a year, the tuitions of the proposed seventy apprentices would bring a much-needed infusion of capital. The apprentices would work in the studio and in the fields, combining both architectural study and physical labor. They would learn about design and construction literally from the ground up, active in all phases of the business; in addition, they would have the experience of working with one of the renowned American masters.

A CHAIR DESIGNED BY FRANK LLOYD WRIGHT FOR THE DANA-THOMAS HOUSE IN SPRINGFIELD, ILLINOIS, 1902.

The idea for the fellowship was not a new one. In almost all of its features, the program reflected the philosophy of the Hillside Home School established by Wright's aunts nearly forty years earlier, which was itself merely an application of ancient ideas brought to America by the Lloyd-Jones clan. Indeed, many people have commented that the closest equivalent of the Taliesin Fellowship was a medieval manorial estate.

Perhaps the first lesson learned by the earliest apprentices at Taliesin was that nothing stayed the same for long. Despite the rigid rules Wright and Olgivanna devised to run the establishment, everything revolved around the pragmatic realities of living on a farm during the Depression, the pressures to develop creative designs, and the personal whims of Mr. Wright.

Edgar Tafel was among the first apprentices. In 1932 he was an architectural student at New York University, when one morning his aunt handed him a clipping from the *Herald Tribune* announcing that Wright was starting his own school of architecture. Tafel had already become mesmerized by Wright's ideas after reading his autobiography and a volume of Wright's lectures delivered at Princeton University. He sat down and wrote a letter to Wright, explaining how much he would like to join the Fellowship but that he had only $450. Two long weeks passed before Tafel received a telegram from Spring Green: "BELIEVE WE CAN MANAGE A FELLOWSHIP FOR YOU IF YOU PAY ALL YOU CAN NOW STOP YOU MAY COME NOW INTO TEMPORARY QUARTERS . . . FRANK LLOYD WRIGHT."

The native New Yorker took a train to Chicago and a bus to the little town of Spring Green, which then had a population of about four hundred. At the bus station he found someone driving out to Taliesin, caught a ride in the rumble seat, and was soon deposited with his bags at the site of the old Hillside Home School. There was Wright in the gymnasium he had designed years before, standing by a piano and listening to a wind-up phonograph screeching out a Beethoven symphony. Tafel walked over and said, "Mr. Wright, I'm Edgar Tafel. From New York."

Wright shook the hand of the nervous student and replied, "Young man, help me move this piano." Before the day was over Tafel was already busy at work at Taliesin. His first task after moving the piano was whitewashing bathrooms.

The first apprentices at Taliesin helped prepare the quarters for those that followed. When the second wave appeared, they began constructing the studio they would work in. Building, renovating and rebuilding was a constant at Taliesin. Students learned about building by digging foundations; excavating sand; burning lime for plaster, mortar, and concrete; cutting timber; constructing the buildings; and making cabinets, shelves, trim, doors, windows, and furniture. In addition, the fellows, especially in the early years, took turns in the fields and gardens. Those who already had farm experience were sometimes given extra jobs of milking cows and cleaning stables. During harvest everyone, including Wright and Olgivanna, worked in the fields and threshed grain or husked corn. The small farm was thus able to grow most of its own food and occasionally raised a surplus. When this happened, Wright would fill his car with baskets of tomatoes, string beans, and peas and drive to Madison to sell them. He was rarely able to get a good price, however, since many others during the middle of the depression were trying to do the same thing.

The nation's economic slump created numerous hardships for the Wrights' large extended family. Everyone at Taliesin became used to "making do or doing without." Wright himself became skilled at bargaining with merchants and local governmental agencies for tools, materials, and even food and clothing. Electricity was provided by a generator that ran only when necessary in order to conserve energy. Whenever the fellowship was forced to hire an electrician or plumber, a student would closely follow him everywhere he went, quietly watching and learning his trade. Soon the apprentices could do almost all the wiring and plumbing at Taliesin.

During the Great Depression, Wright was even reduced, upon occasion, to calling up old friends and clients to beg for money. Eventually he could no longer even pay for the long-distance phone charges. Trips by automobile during this time were often on back roads, on worn-out tires, for Wright could pay for neither license plates nor new tires. The bottom

FRANK LLOYD WRIGHT WITH STUDENTS AT TALIESIN, 1937.

seemed to hit when Wright decided to do away with lunch at the fellow-ship. Olgivanna stepped in at this point and suggested to her husband, "Well, Frank, why don't we just have bread and milk?" Soon other items were added to the noon menu as well.

Wright seemed very little affected by these annoyances. In fact, he seemed sometimes to revel in them, viewing them merely as challenges to be overcome. The creative life was not supposed to be a comfortable

OVERLEAF: *FRANK LLOYD WRIGHT'S DRAWING OF FALLINGWATER, WHICH IS PROBABLY THE MOST FAMOUS MODERN HOUSE IN THE WORLD.*

one. Life at Taliesin, even after prosperity returned, was never without its inconveniences, many of them created by Wright himself. The daily schedule was constantly being reorganized. Plans carefully plotted one evening would be swept away in the morning. An apprentice could wake up in Spring Green one day and, without any previous notice, find himself going to bed that night at a job site a hundred miles away.

Life at Taliesin was a mirror of Wright's creative life itself. It was a constant chaos out of which Wright continually created order. When an apprentice watching him work brought to Wright's attention that he was designing outside the grid lines plotted on a piece of paper, Wright shot back, "I'm not going to be a slave to the grid just because I invented it."

Corrections were not done only on paper. Wright was never entirely satisfied, and he never considered one of his designs complete. He was always moving furniture around in clients' houses, and even in houses he just happened to be visiting. Sometimes his adjustments were more extensive. One day Wright appeared unannounced at the home of one client in California who was in the midst of entertaining some of his friends with a barbecue. Wright emerged from his car with several of his apprentices and, before he had even said hello to his host, pointed his cane toward a wall he didn't like. "Rip it out," he commanded, and his apprentices immediately went to work tearing down the offensive structure. (Wright, in compensation, left four apprentices, who boarded with the new homeowners for a month while they built a more appropriate wall.)

This was not just the idiosyncrasy of a creative genius. Wright's ability to imagine his life and his work in a perpetual state of becoming was a source of strength that he brought to everything he did. His toleration of disorder was at the core of his creative philosophy.

Olgivanna Wright, during these years, acted as a keel to Wright's sometimes wandering vessel. She brought to the fellowship some degree of the common sense that Wright sometimes lacked. Often as headstrong as her husband, she offered the apprentices another ear and frequently brought their concerns to Wright, knowing just the right word and the right time to direct his actions in a practical course. Along with her many talents, she brought to Taliesin her experiences in group living and creative expression from her stay with Georgi Gurdjieff's Institute for the Harmonious Development of Man in Paris. With her daughters, Svetlana and Iovanna, she directed the smooth operation of the fellowship's immediate daily needs, but few people failed to understand that she was a dynamic force in every activity undertaken by Wright.

Many of the apprentices at Taliesin, especially in its later years, chafed at what they saw as Wright's capriciousness, and Olgivanna's severity. Life in the close-knit community was not for everyone, but many people who came there thrived and blossomed as individuals in ways it is unlikely they would have otherwise. Edgar Tafel, who came to Taliesin thinking he would stay only for a year or two, remained for nine years. His career there began with moving a piano and ended with him designing buildings on his own and splitting the profits with the foundation. William Wesley Peters, who, like Tafel, arrived at Taliesin the first year of the fellowship, married Svetlana and worked with Wright and later with the Frank Lloyd Wright Foundation until he died in 1992. John Howe, who also came to Taliesin in 1932, after earning his first year's tuition of three-hundred dollars by setting up pins at a Chicago bowling alley, oversaw activities in the drafting room for more than thirty years. Eugene Masselink, Wright's personal secretary, became the chief director of the publications program at Taliesin. Bruce Brooks Pfeiffer joined the fellowship relatively late, in 1949, and still serves as foundation archivist. Many others came to Taliesin and, whether they stayed a short time or a long time, gained a new awareness of their creative potential.

For many of Wright's apprentices, their stay at Taliesin was marked by the warmth of a large and caring, if often chaotic and sometimes restricting, community. They remembered the home-cooked meals, the bread and cakes hot out of the oven. They remembered the Sunday picnics, which Wright, like his Uncle Jenkin years before, would close with a few words of wisdom—but which were usually about organic architecture rather than religion. They remembered the dramatic performances and the movies in the theater at Taliesin, or the music performed by the fellowship string quartet or choir. Everyone was encouraged to participate, not just in the studio, but in all aspects of life at Taliesin.

Wright's experiences during the Depression years led him to an enlarged social vision, one, perhaps, he would not have understood during his prosperous and thriving years in Oak Park and Chicago. He began to see architecture more and more in terms of its larger social context. A just and humane society was not just the result of abstract political philosophies; it was something that had to be constructed out of the daily lives of a people. Architecture had an important, maybe the most important, role in helping to form such a society.

Wright believed that the evils of modern society, which had brought on the Great Depression, were all associated with the modern city. In his book, *The Disappearing City* (1932), Wright first outlined his vision of the modern city as "a parasite of the spirit." Cities, Wright argued, were the source of everything that had gone wrong in America. The concentrations of humanity on a limited amount of land allowed greedy landlords and bankers to extract the maximum amount of profit out of the lives of unfortunate urban dwellers. The credit system, so removed from its roots in a natural, organic economy, led inevitably to commercial and industrial overexpansion, unemployment, and military adventurism. The 1929 crash and the clouds of war, which Wright and others could see forming on the distant horizon throughout the 1930s, seemed to Wright to be the proof of his critique of the city.

Many of these ideas were not unique to Wright. They formed a major theme of intellectual and political discussion in the thirties. It was an especially strong sentiment in the American heartland, which still saw World War I as an unnecessary and futile conflict. Wright's friends Robert La Follette and Phil La Follette (who was the secretary of Frank Lloyd Wright Incorporated) worked vigorously as governor and senator of Wisconsin to advance these populist and progressive ideals. To Wright the solution to the problems confronting America lay in a radically new relationship between people and their environment. The city, Wright believed, was dying. It was being made obsolete every day by the new communications and transportation systems that allowed a greater dispersion of the population. True democracy, Wright believed, required the elimination of cities and the artificial boundaries of states and towns. In 1935, he set his apprentices to the task of building a model of such an ideal community.

The model of Broadacre City, as he called it, was a twelve-by-twelve-foot representation of a four-square-mile section of a decentralized and restructured nation. It was not a city, village, or town but a part of a continuum, as if an arbitrary section had been cut from a larger geographical context. Perhaps the basic archetype of Broadacre City was found by Wright, not in political and social theories, but in the philosophy of forms and voids that Wright's architecture shared with traditional Japanese aesthetics. For Broadacre City, as for a Japanese rock garden or a wood block print, the significance of the design lay not merely in the objects in a landscape or the marks on a page but in the spaces they defined. Wright frequently cited Lao Tze who proposed that "the reality of a vessel was the void within it." This was the philosophy that lay behind every building which Wright designed, and behind the ideal social community

ABOVE: *FRANK LLOYD WRIGHT'S PENCIL DRAWING OF THE HERBERT JACOBS HOUSE, MADISON, WISCONSIN, HIS FIRST USONIAN HOUSE, 1937.*

OPPOSITE: *FALLINGWATER, AS IT STANDS TODAY IN BEAR RUN, PENNSYLVANIA.*

he envisioned. Broadacre had no major monument; perhaps its primary feature was the arterial roadway that lay at the periphery of the model. Here were clustered separate highways for cars and trucks, a high-speed monorail, and continuous warehousing. Nearby were businesses, markets, pollution-free industries, and hotels. Dispersed around this area were parks, farms, vineyards, schools, and homes. Each home was designed so that it could be partly built out of prefabricated materials by the family itself, and each house had a minimum of an acre of ground, to allow space for a family vegetable garden.

In 1935, Wright's Broadacre City model was exhibited in the most incongruous place imaginable—Rockefeller Center, in the heart of metropolitan Manhattan. Many critics, then and since, have snickered at Wright's idealistic utopia. For centuries visionaries have imagined shining cities with spectacular buildings reaching toward the heavens, or they have dreamed of "back to the earth" agrarian communities. But Wright's ideal was not a city, was not the country, and was not a suburb. It was a piece of a larger fabric, a decentralized network of homes, businesses, industries, farms, and roads. As farfetched as Wright's ideas sounded in the 1930s and for many years thereafter, America today, with interstate highways, suburban shopping malls, and its commercial strips, looks a lot like the Broadacre City Wright designed in 1935.

Wright's designs for an ideal community were not limited to the drawing board. Some architectural historians have argued that everything Wright built was a part of Broadacre City, and that through his influence on others, he more than anyone else, transformed the fabric of the American landscape. Perhaps one of the most influential, but certainly not one of the best known, buildings Wright ever designed, was the house he built for newspaper reporter Herbert Jacobs and his wife, Katherine.

The Jacobses had been looking for a house near Madison, Wisconsin, they could afford on a reporter's salary. They were thinking of something in the Dutch Colonial style with white painted bricks. As it happened, Katherine Jacobs's cousin was an artist who had spent a summer at Taliesin. She suggested that they ask Wright to design a house. The Jacobs thought that Wright would work only for millionaires, but nevertheless they drove to Spring Green and nervously announced to the architect, "What this country needs is a decent five-thousand dollar house. Can you design one for us?" To their surprise, Wright agreed.

The result was Wright's first "Usonian" House. The name was a play on "USA" for a home for a new America. It looked nothing like a Dutch Colonial, but many of the innovations introduced in the Jacobses' home would become standard features in houses throughout the country. The Usonian House was built on a concrete slab that contained the building's heating system—wrought-iron steam pipes. Later, copper tubing would be used for hot water. This radiant, or "gravity," system allowed an even heat rising from the floor, eliminating unsightly radiators as well as drafts. As an unforeseen advantage, it kept dogs and cats off the furniture—they preferred curling up on the floor. Since the Jacobses had no servants, the kitchen was not pushed out to a wing of the house but was located in the center of the home, where Mrs. Jacobs could prepare dinner while she watched her children or conversed with guests. Wright was successful in adapting some of the features of the Prairie House, such as flat roofs, open plans, and access to the outdoors, while still maintaining the family's privacy, for a house with a modest price. The Jacobs' house was one of Wright's designs that was actually built within its budget. The Jacobses perhaps even came out a little ahead by charging fifty cents admission to curious visitors.

The Usonian House was studied by thousands of architects either in person or through articles about it that appeared in *Life* magazine and *Architectural Forum* in 1938. Alfred Levitt left his job for six months in 1937 to observe the construction of a Usonian House in Great Neck, New York. He incorporated many of its features in the cape and ranch style houses his firm built in Levittown, Long Island, creating what many believed was a monumental eyesore, but at the same time initiating a revolution in residential home construction. The Wright designs, reinterpreted by the Levitt construction company, are the basis for nearly every post–World War II housing development in the country.

"But let us go in. This man who respects nature, we see, is a lover of flowers and growing things, because, to be a normally growing thing is to be beautiful, and while his piece of ground is small, he arranges and subdivides that too with a sympathetic eye and hand to harmonize with his plan, so that his building and his ground are not finally separable, one from the other; you scarcely know where ground leaves off and building begins. So we approach nearer the heart of this gently developing scheme and wait for the door to open."

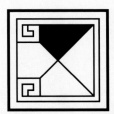

■

CHAPTER SEVEN

SECOND FLOWERING

Hitler's rise to power in Germany during the 1930s would have almost as dramatic an impact on Frank Lloyd Wright and American architecture as on every other aspect of American life. A generation of young German architects was scattered throughout the world, fleeing from the repressions of Nazi Germany. Many of them were first introduced to America through an exhibition of their work at the Museum of Modern Art in New York. The exhibit of "international architects" (which also included the works of Wright) was one of those critical events that defined the course of American architectural history. Individual architects who participated in the 1932 exhibition, such as Walter Gropius, Ludwig Mies van der Rohe, and Le Corbusier, over the course of nearly half a century would virtually reshape the American city. The architects of

the International style, as they became known, had much in common with Wright. Most of them had been profoundly influenced by his work, which they had become familiar with in Germany through the Wasmuth portfolios of 1910. Indeed, Wright's fame had spread throughout Europe while he was still relatively unknown in the United States. The younger generation of European architects had been especially inspired by Wright's rebelliousness; his anti-classicism; his attempts to design in harmony with the new technologies of steel, glass, and concrete; and his (and Sullivan's) emphasis on the harmony of form and function. A new genera-

tion of American architects and architectural critics would be introduced Wright's work and philosophy by such architects as Mies van der Rohe and Gropius who joined the faculties of major American universities.

Yet there were some striking contrasts between Wright and his foreign admirers. They took, for example, Sullivan's dictum that "form follows function" much more seriously and literally than did Wright. The new architects made a virtual religion out of functionalism, often losing sight of the responsibility of architecture to reflect the intangible needs of its occupants. As Le Corbusier expressed it, houses were simply "machines for living."

The Johnson Wax Administration Building and Research Tower.

INTERIOR OF THE JOHNSON WAX BUILDING. THE TWENTY-FOOT-HIGH CEILING IS SUPPORTED BY COLUMNS THAT FLARE OUT INTO LARGE CIRCLES. PYREX GLASS TUBING ALLOWS DAYLIGHT TO POUR DOWN INTO THE WORK AREA BELOW.

To Wright the machine-inspired aesthetic of the Internationalists simply led back to an old, and antihumanistic, rationalism, which he had long criticized in its ancient costume of classicism. The new architects seemed to Wright to be committing the same sins that he had found fault with in the generation that preceded them. They were again creating an architecture of boxes. Some of those, especially the glass boxes of Mies van der Rohe, were admittedly beautiful, abstract designs. But the Internationalists were guilty, as Wright described it, of designing from the outside in, rather than organically from the inside out.

The Internationalists believed that they were developing a democratic, people's architecture. Some of their earliest designs were for workers' housing in pre-war Germany, and many of them, especially Gropius, believed that architecture should be the result of a collaborative process, rather than the invention of a single creative individual. Such thinking was anathema to Wright. These philosophies seemed to him to lead to a bland conformity and reeked of the totalitarianism that the architects of the International style themselves were fleeing. Wright's idea of the relationship of the individual to the larger society was fundamentally different. Democracy did not mean, to Wright, a leveling of everything to the lowest common denominator. It was characterized instead by the progress of individuals to realize their fullest potential.

Relations between Wright and the architects of the International style were often strained. Public groups frequently brought them together as representatives of the new modern style of architecture, and at such forums, the atmosphere was generally polite and cordial. Wright constantly insisted, however, both publicly and privately, that whatever was good in the work of the Internationalists was the result of his influence. Maybe he was right.

Of all the architects working in the International style, Wright probably had the closest relationship with Ludwig Mies van der Rohe, who taught at the Illinois Institute of Technology and whose work so dramatically altered the Chicago skyline. When Mies first came to Chicago, some of his friends called Wright (Mies could not yet speak English) and asked if they could drop by for a visit. Wright agreed, and Mies and two companions arrived at Taliesin for lunch the same day. His friends went back to Chicago that afternoon. Not until four days later, however, would Mies finally be returned to Chicago, after a visit to Wright's studio and a grand tour of local projects designed by Wright which were then in progress. According to the foundation archivist,

Bruce Brooks Pfeiffer, Mies van der Rohe's translator sometimes added his own critical evaluations of Wright's buildings while on the tour. Finally Mies interrupted him, blurting out, "Be quiet, you are in the presence of genius."

Edgar Tafel, who acted as chauffeur during the visit, described the differences between Wright and Mies van der Rohe: "Mies dedicated his entire life to the search for one style, refining and purifying. . . . Wright kept evolving, growing, and developing new styles." For Wright, "what we did yesterday, we won't do today. And what we don't do tomorrow will not be what we'll be doing the day after." Mies van der Rohe's philosophy was just the opposite. "You don't start a new style each Monday," he argued.

Wright never waited for Monday; he didn't have the time. In 1936, Wright entered his seventieth year. In that year he designed the most modest, and the most impressive, houses of his career—the Usonian House for Herbert Jacobs and Fallingwater for Edgar Kaufmann. The same year, he designed the corporate headquarters for Johnson Wax Company. Wright's long period of commercial inactivity was ending. The long years marked by tragedy, scandal, impoverishment, and professional inactivity had helped to create in Wright a new social vision and a burst of imaginative energy that would not abate with age. Now, finally, he began to gain the commercial success and recognition that had long eluded him.

The breakthrough that launched Wright's "second career" was the Johnson Wax administration building. In many ways it continued themes and innovations first conceived in Wright's earliest architecture. Like the Larkin Building, the Johnson Wax building contained a large, open room for office workers, ringed by a balcony. Wright, in addition, continued the experiments in reinforced concrete he had begun at Unity Temple in Oak Park. He brought to the new structure, however, some dramatic ideas that once again proved his mastery of space and technology. Perhaps most remarkable is the large, open-plan office space (128 feet by 208 feet), with its twenty-foot high ceiling supported by dendriform columns that flare out into large circles to support Pyrex glass tubing, so daylight pours down into the work area below. The effect on the observer has been described as being like swimming in a large pool with water-lily pads floating above.

"The most famous modern house in the world," Fallingwater, was designed by Wright for the wealthy department-store magnate Edgar J.

Kaufmann. E. J., as Wright called him, had learned of Wright's work when his son, Edgar Kaufmann, Jr., went to Taliesin in 1934 as an apprentice. Before the year was out, Wright was involved in a number of important works for Kaufmann. This was not an ordinary client, however. Over the years Wright and the elder Kaufmann would become close friends. Their work together on Fallingwater was almost as much a collaboration as an independent commission. Kaufmann's role was more like a patron of the arts, a Renaissance merchant prince, directing as well as employing the talents of his craftsman. Kaufmann's greatest genius, however, lay in recognizing and giving virtual free rein to Wright's own genius.

The Kaufmann family had long vacationed in their rustic retreat along Bear Run in western Pennsylvania. Edgar and his wife, Liliane, particularly enjoyed swimming in the pools and sunbathing on the boulders surrounding a waterfall that cascaded through the forest of rhododendrons, mountain laurels, pine trees, and oaks. Now they asked Wright to design a house that would take advantage of the unique qualities of the site.

Wright visited Bear Run late in 1934 and asked Kaufmann to have a topographic map of the area sent to him. For nine months Wright thought about the designs for the house but put nothing on paper. One morning he received a call from Kaufmann, who said he was just leaving Milwaukee for Taliesin to look at the plans. Wright went to his studio and sat down at his drawing board, while two of his assistants, Edgar Tafel and Bob Mosher, frantically replaced colored pencils, that were used up as fast as they were sharpened. Mesmerized, they watched Wright, talking to himself, lay out the plans for the house. "Liliane and E.J. will have tea on the balcony . . . . They'll cross the bridge to walk into the woods . . . . The rock on which E. J. sits will be the hearth, coming right out of the floor, the fire burning just behind it . . . ." His pencil would break, and Tafel or Mosher would hand him another.

When Kaufmann arrived around lunchtime, the plans looked as though they had been completed for weeks. He looked at them, surprised. He had expected a house with a view of the falls. Wright had designed a house on the falls. The house as it was finally built was almost exactly as Wright had laid it out that morning. Dynamic cantilevered, reinforced-concrete terraces jutted out over the falls. The boulder, E.J.'s favorite place to sun himself, was built into the house, becoming the hearthstone of the central fireplace. Steps from the living room led down to a plunge pool for quick dips.

It is a superb technological achievement. Scores of engineers inspected the house and the site at every stage of its construction and predicted that the cantilevers would fail, the waters would destroy the foundation, the falls themselves would recede, and the building would collapse. Fallingwater has withstood storms, snowfalls, and floods for over half a century and, with minor repairs and renovations, remains as stable today as when it was built. The house has become one of the most photographed structures in the world. Many pictures reproduce the dramatic beauty of the design, but all fail to suggest the fundamental character of the house. It is as much a feeling as a monument. It expresses a search for harmony between man and nature, which began when mankind first started down the path toward civilized society, and which perhaps comes as near its end as possible at Fallingwater.

"And I warn Henry [Hitchcock] right here and now that, having a good start, not only do I fully intend to be the greatest architect who has yet lived, but fully intend to be the greatest architect who will ever live. Yes, I intend to be the greatest architect of all time."

■

CHAPTER EIGHT

FRANK LLOYD WRIGHT, ARCHITECT OF AN AGE

As early as 1927, Frank Lloyd Wright and Olgivanna began an annual winter expedition from Taliesin in Wisconsin to Arizona. He was first called there to help a former apprentice, Albert C. McArthur, with designs for the new Arizona Biltmore. The following year Wright, Olgivanna, and their two daughters traveled with a small staff to work on another projected hotel near Phoenix. This second hotel was never built. It was one of a number of projects that Wright was working on when the stockmarket crash occurred in 1929 and that were never completed. The trip became an unexpected success, however, as a result of one of Wright's erratic attempts at frugality. To save money, he decided that the small contingent would camp in the desert rather than rent rooms in a nearby hotel. The desert campsite, named Ocatillo, became an experimental laboratory for concepts and technologies that Wright would apply

Svetlana, Iovanna, Olgivanna, and Frank Lloyd Wright parked in front of Ocatillo, Chandler, Arizona, 1928.

in constructions throughout the rest of his career. With only the most basic materials—desert stone, redwood, and canvas—Wright was able to create a small community of buildings that seemed a natural expression of the starkly beautiful landscape.

In 1938, with the profits from his recent professional achievements, Wright purchased eight hundred acres of public land in Scottsdale, near Phoenix. Taliesin West, as Wright called his newest home, was his final great adventure in living in an organic building structure. Like all of his homes, it was never completed; it was always in a state of evolution. The constant building and rebuilding that had begun with his home in Oak Park, continued in Spring Green, and now resumed in Scottsdale. Taliesin West, throughout Wright's life and even today, has much of the impermanent character of the desert camp established in 1928. The entire site comes as close as it is possible, perhaps, to seeing Wright's thoughts stopped in time as if the sun itself, in its traverse across the desert sky, had suddenly halted in a frozen, timeless moment.

BELOW: *TALIESIN WEST, FRANK LLOYD WRIGHTS'S STUDIO AND HOME IN SCOTTSDALE, ARIZONA. BUILT BY WRIGHT AND HIS APPRENTICES, IT BEGAN AS A DESERT CAMP AND EVOLVED AS A STRUCTURE WITH MASONRY WALLS, REDWOOD RAFTERS, AND ADJUSTABLE CANVAS BLINDS, WHICH WERE FINALLY REPLACED BY STEEL, GLASS, AND PLASTIC.*

During the final years of Wright's life, he worked at a pace and with an intensity that suggested he was making up for the long years of enforced idleness. He completed the designs and, with his apprentices, oversaw the construction of dozens of new commissions each year— houses, churches, theaters, stores. Each was seemingly more brilliant and startling than the last. In addition to the structures he completed, Wright left hundreds of plans that were never built. They give us only a glimpse of the incredible possibilities that might have found expression had funds been more available, clients more daring, his own life longer.

Among those unbuilt designs were the plans for a mile-high building; one of Wright's most quixotic projects. In an era in which many noted architects had become famous for their skyscrapers, Wright was a constant critic of these buildings that allowed unscrupulous landlords to extract exorbitant rents from hapless city-dwellers. Wright pleaded incessantly for an architecture in harmony with its natural environment. He had become famous for houses whose horizontal lines expressed his organic philosophy of building. How could he propose a mile-high office building?

It was all, perhaps, to prove a point. Every obstacle to Wright was merely a challenge. He would admit that nothing was beyond his reach. A mile-high building, Wright argued, would allow for the densest possible concentration of people and would consequently yield a vast amount of surrounding space which could be utilized for more dispersed and horizontal structures. It may not have been an entirely convincing argument, but the major importance of the plan perhaps lay in the conception of its execution. It would essentially be like an enormous plant with a huge tap-root anchoring it firmly to the earth. The 528 floors would be cantilevered out from the central stalk like the branches of a tree. This old idea of building would be united with the newest technology (circa 1956). Cars could be parked in underground parking lots, helicopters would land on terraces, and individuals would be transported from floor to floor in atomic-powered elevators. It was not an entirely preposterous idea. In principle it could, perhaps, be accomplished. Wright himself had used the basic construction ideas in a tower he built as an addition to the Johnson Wax Building in 1944 and in the original plans for the Price Company Tower in Bartlesville, Oklahoma (constructed in 1952). To Wright, the mile-high office building was an expression of the same organic philosophy that was the basis of all of his work.

Perhaps Wright's last great design, however, was not for a skyscraper but for a museum in the heart of Manhattan. The Solomon R.

Guggenheim Museum had been on Wright's drawing boards for years before construction began, and it was opened to the public shortly after Wright's death in 1959. Solomon Guggenheim's sole stipulation, when he awarded the commission to Wright, was that the building for his collection of nonobjective art be like no other museum in the world. The Guggenheim is certainly that.

Essentially it is an inverted cone, like a gigantic, squat ice-cream cone. Visitors take an elevator to the top and amble down a gentle, spiraling ramp, viewing artworks in the process. Starkly modern when it was completed in 1959, many of its characteristic features—the use of poured concrete, an open atrium, a dramatic walkway—can be seen in his earliest work in Unity Temple, the Larkin Building, and the Charnley House. Those ideas were coupled here with the circular theme that dominated much of Wright's latest work.

The Guggenheim Museum has never lacked its chorus of critics. Architectural pundits have described the building as a beehive with gun slits, and have criticized the lighting and the angled wall plane, which they argue is unsuited for the display of paintings. Wright and his defenders have argued each of the critics' points. The natural light and the angled walls, they say, recreate the conditions in an artist's studio, where paintings are supported on angled easels. Even if the critics were correct, however, the fact remains that the building has done more to bring viewers to study and appreciate modern art than could have been hoped for with any other structure. When the museum first opened its doors, thousands of people lined up for blocks to enter, and crowds have continued to come ever since to examine both the artworks on display and the great piece of art that houses them.

Wright never saw the finished building. Six months before the Guggenheim opened, Frank Lloyd Wright, age ninety-one years, died on April 9, 1959. He had complained of stomach pains a few days earlier and was transported from Taliesin West to Saint Joseph's Hospital in Phoenix. An operation for an intestinal blockage was successful, but accompanying hemorrhaging weakened the patient beyond his ability to recover. His body was transported to Spring Green, where a service was held and two hundred mourners followed as the casket was carried in a horse-drawn farm wagon to the chapel Wright had helped design many years earlier. There his body was laid to rest with his many Lloyd-Jones ancestors. In 1985 his remains were disinterred, cremated, and reburied with those of Olgivanna's at Taliesin West. Wright's personality and his

THE MILE HIGH "ILLINOIS" BUILDING PROJECT THAT FRANK LLOYD WRIGHT PRESENTED IN 1956, SO-CALLED BECAUSE HE INTENDED THAT ALL THE OFFICIAL DEPARTMENTS OF THE STATE OF ILLINOIS SHOULD BE HOUSED IN IT. IT HAD 528 FLOORS, A STACK OF FIVE TERRACES, AND A GROUND LEVEL FOR PARKING CARS AND HELICOPTERS.

MODERN GALLERY
SEUM FOR THE SOLOMON R GUGGENHEIM FOUNDATION
FRANK LLOYD WRIGHT ARCHITECT
HOLDEN, AND McLAUGHLIN ASSOCIATES

ABOVE: ONE OF FRANK LLOYD WRIGHT'S DRAWINGS OF THE SOLOMON R. GUGGENHEIM MUSEUM, NEW YORK CITY, 1959. THE INTERIOR IS A SPIRALING RAMP, ALONG THE WALLS OF WHICH WORKS OF ART ARE EXHIBITED. THIS SHAPE CREATES A GALLERY THAT IS UNIFIED AND CONTINUOUS— ALL THE SPACE RELATING TO THE WHOLE.

These drawings are Frank Lloyd Wright's designs for a helicopter (above) and a "road machine" (opposite). The helicopter was to be radio controlled and self-steering. It was to rest in a type of socket landing dock, with its entrance doors level with the station platform on the ground level or roof terraces of a building. The "road machine" was to be a taxicab, with a separate compartment for the driver above the passengers, where the view of the road would be unimpeded.

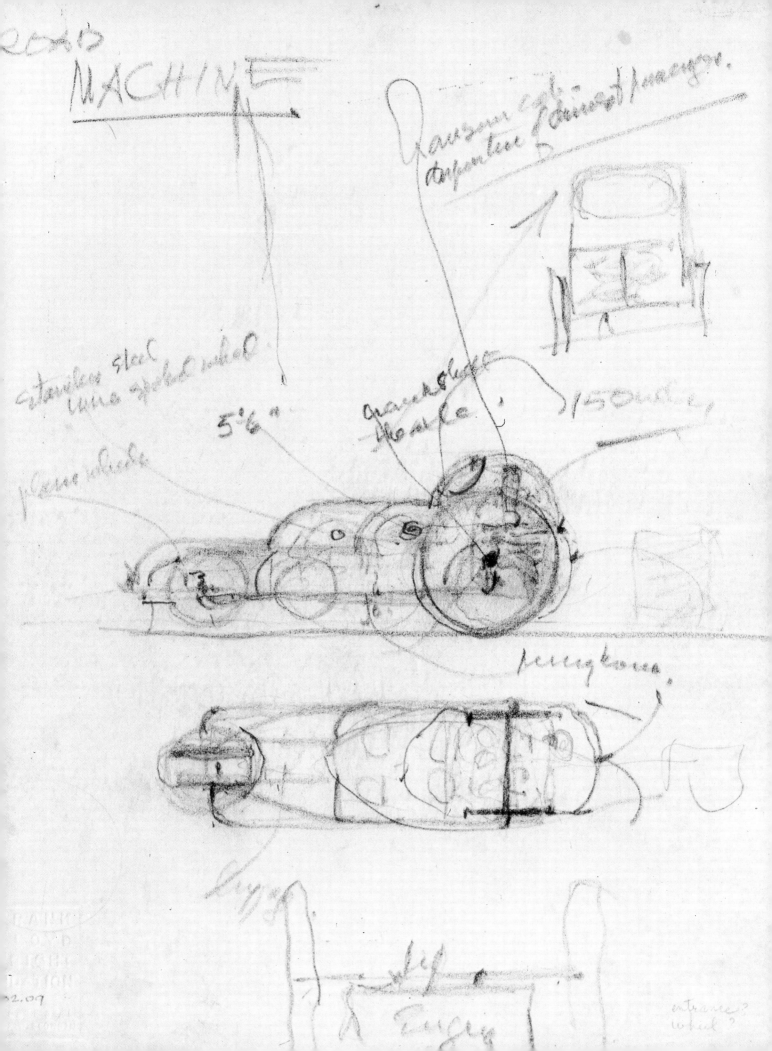

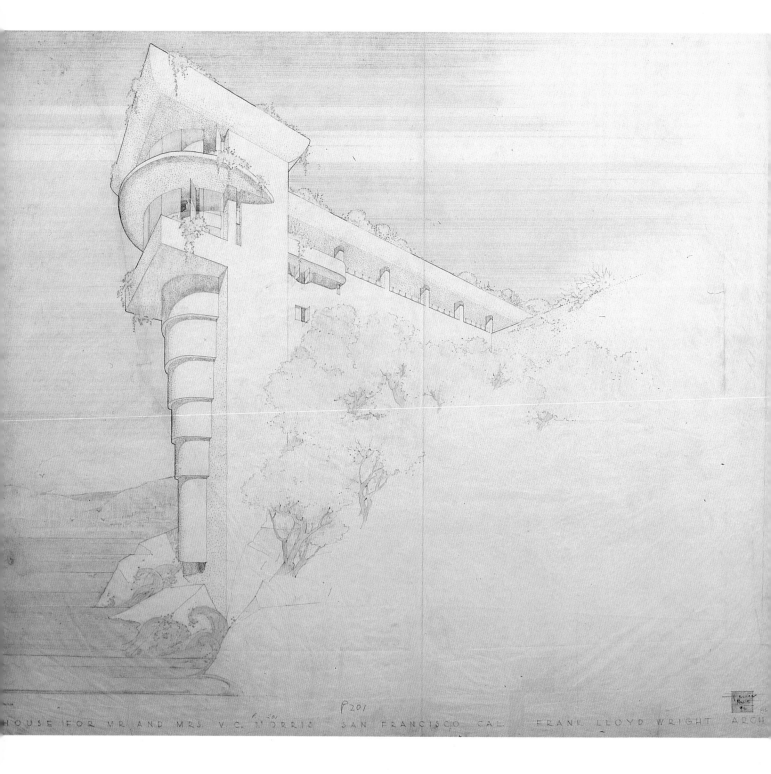

P 201

HOUSE FOR MR. AND MRS. V. C. MORRIS   SAN FRANCISCO, CAL.   FRANK LLOYD WRIGHT   ARCH

"So every true building is of the quality of some man's soul, his sense of harmony and 'fitness,' which is another kind of harmony—more or less manifest in the fallible human process. And his building will nobly stand, belonging to its site— breathing this message to the spirit quite naturally, so long as his work was well done or the course of human events does not inundate or human ignorance willfully destroy his building."

OPPOSITE: "SEACLIFF," THE V. C. MORRIS HOUSE PROJECT, 1945. THIS HOUSE WAS TO BE ON THE CLIFF NEAR THE GOLDEN GATE BRIDGE IN SAN FRANCISCO. WRIGHT STACKED THE LIVING QUARTERS VERTICALLY TO CREATE A HOME THAT IS PART OF THE CLIFF ITSELF. THE REINFORCED CONCRETE ROOF EDGES ABOVE THE TOP LEVEL TURN UP TO HOLD SOIL FOR A ROOF GARDEN.

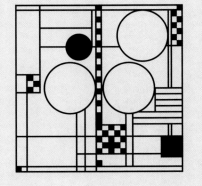

philosophy, however, have not yet come to rest. Journalists and critics still sift through the bones of his life, like ancient soothsayers trying to detect patterns and meanings. One overwhelming characteristic of his life is always mentioned: Frank Lloyd Wright was one of the most arrogant individuals in American cultural history. Once when he testified at a legal proceeding, he was asked by the judge if he considered himself the greatest architect of all time. He is reported to have responded, "yes." Later, when he was asked how he could be so egotistical, he replied, "But I was under oath."

It is often suggested that, to Wright, his creative genius was more important than his clients' wishes or comfort. Wright's beautifully designed furniture, similarly, was a testament to his genius but sometimes not very functional. His three-legged chairs at the Johnson Wax Building were constantly throwing secretaries to the floor. Wright himself admitted that he had become black-and-blue from too intimate contact with his own furniture. These stories have grown with the telling and retelling, and perhaps illustrate Wright's sense of humor as much as his arrogance. To a large degree such monumental egotism was itself a pose, part of the job responsibilities that went with being America's most renowned architect. His clients have nearly universally praised his ability to listen to their wishes and to incorporate their ideas into the final designs. Wright was a genius of, if nothing else, pleasing his clients. Still, he realized very early in life that, as he put it, an honest arrogance was preferable to a hypocritical humility. Truth was always the most important virtue to Wright.

Wright's larger role in American cultural history is similarly the cause of controversy. During his life Wright was continually the iconoclast and a relentless social critic. "The United States," he quoted Georges Clemenceau "was the only nation to pass from barbarism to degeneracy never having known a civilization." He castigated both the architecture and the social life of American cities. He excoriated the unequal distribution of wealth and criticized "private ownership and the profit system." Before World War II he had been an ardent isolationist, convinced that accommodations could be made between America, Germany, and Japan. After the war he continued to preach for understanding of America's enemies, now represented by the Soviet Union, and he defended the trip to Russia he made in 1937. During the cold war he advocated unilateral nuclear disarmament and supported pacifism.

All of this activity did not go unnoticed. The House Un-American Activities Committee placed Wright on one of its famous lists of

Americans affiliated with "Communist front organizations." Not surprisingly, Wright never received a government contract during his lifetime of creative work. Wright, however, was neither a communist nor a socialist. He would not belong to any group, as he said, with an "ist" or "ism" after its name. Politically as well as architecturally, Wright was essentially a radical advocating a complete restructuring of the status quo. Probably no political system would have pleased him—but that was not the point. For Wright the goal was neither a finished system of government nor the completed structure of a building. It was the process that was of first interest and importance to Wright. The goal was continual improvement, unending progress, which could not be accomplished by complacency or apathy. The role of architecture in this process was paramount, even more significant than the role of politics. As Wright himself said, "I don't build a house without predicting the end of the present social order."

If Wright was un-American, however, so was Thomas Jefferson, with whom he had so much in common and whom he frequently cited. The third president is perhaps the only American architect of equivalent stature to Frank Lloyd Wright, and the similarities between their work and their ideas of society are striking. Jefferson's Monticello and Wright's Fallingwater are the two greatest monuments of American residential architecture. Not incidentally, both Jefferson and Wright rejected the monumental, picture-book quality of the buildings by their contemporaries. Both built geometrically complex buildings with subtle spatial organization, hugging the ground and in harmony with their natural surroundings.

Jefferson and Wright also shared a vision of the role of architecture in reforming American society. Each emphasized the necessity for radical change, and imagined both architecture and social reformation as a process, rather than a quest for some static, absolute ideal. Both men ultimately were successful in creating a new architecture for an emerging non-urban middle class. Significantly, Jefferson and Wright held a similar conception of American democracy. They were aristocratic and populist, envisioning a world not of social equality but of equal opportunity, in which individuals could rise to their greatest potential.

Wright's significance in American history is not confined to the structures he designed. Wright was an architect not just of buildings. He was an architect of an age. He did as much as any other person to create the cultural as well as the physical environment of twentieth-century America. His message to us is not always an easy one to understand, let alone to agree with. As Wright's son, John, wrote after his father's death, "My

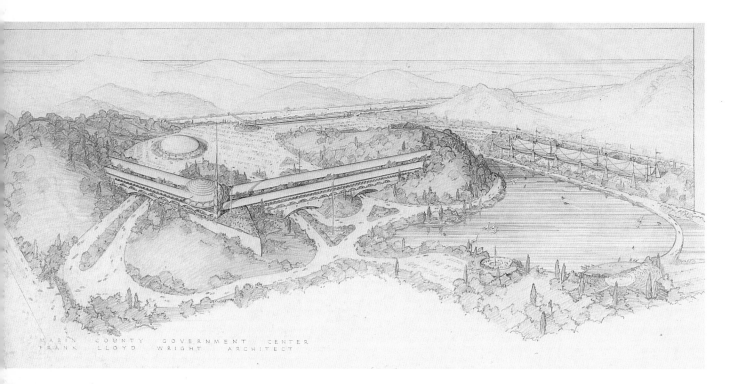

MARIN COUNTY GOVERNMENT CENTER
FRANK LLOYD WRIGHT ARCHITECT

THE MARIN COUNTY CIVIC CENTER, SAN RAPHAEL, CALIFORNIA, 1957. WRIGHT'S DRAWING (ABOVE) SHOWS AN AERIAL PERSPECTIVE OF THE CENTER, WHICH IS A BRIDGE BETWEEN THREE HILLS. THE WINGS ARE DOUBLE ROWS OF OFFICES AND THE SPACE BETWEEN THEM IS COVERED WITH SKYLIGHTS (OPPOSITE) THAT PROVIDE NATURAL LIGHT.

impression of my whole life with him is one of comedy, tragedy, the sublime, the ridiculous, and I never knew where one of them left off and the other began."

Perhaps no one summed up Wright's accomplishments better than Mies van der Rohe, who said of Wright shortly after his death, "In his undiminished power he resembles a giant tree in a wide landscape which year after year attains a more noble crown." The tree still grows in the valley.

OVERLEAF: THE LIVING CITY PROJECT, 1958. FRANK LLOYD WRIGHT WROTE THREE BOOKS ABOUT URBAN DESIGN AND CREATED A TWELVE-FOOT SQUARE MODEL OF BROADACRE CITY, AN URBAN DESIGN OF A CITY INTEGRATED INTO A NATURAL LANDSCAPE. THIS IS ONE OF HIS DRAWINGS OF THE CITY IN PERSPECTIVE. WRIGHT PLACED MANY OF HIS OWN BUILDINGS IN THE SCENE SUCH AS THE MARIN COUNTY CIVIC CENTER AND THE BETH SHOLOM SYNAGOGUE. AT THE BOTTOM HE HAS DRAWN AND LABELED AN "ATOMIC BARGE," AND HIS "TAXI COPTERS" HOVER OVER THE SCENE.

SELECTED EVENTS IN THE LIFE OF
FRANK LLOYD WRIGHT

1867	Frank Lloyd Wright born in Richland Center, Wisconsin, June 8
1874	Wright family moves to Weymouth, Massachusetts
1877	Wright family moves to Madison, Wisconsin
1885	Wright's father files for and is granted a divorce
1886	Wright enters University of Wisconsin as a "special student"
1886–7	Wright moves to Chicago to begin his career in architecture; enters firm of Adler & Sullivan late in 1887; first building of the Hillside Home School, Spring Green, Wisconsin
1889	Wright marries Catherine Tobin and begins building their Oak Park home
1890	Birth of Lloyd, the first of six children
1893	Wright leaves Adler & Sullivan and opens his own office; William Winslow House, River Forest, Illinois
1894	Wright first exhibits work at the Chicago Architectural Club
1901	Frank Thomas House, Oak Park, Illinois, and Ward Willits House, Highland Park, Illinois
1902	Arthur Heurtley House, Oak Park, Illinois
1903	Edwin H. Cheney House, Oak Park, Illinois; Larkin Company Administration Building, Buffalo, New York

1904 Darwin D. Martin House, Buffalo, New York; H. J. Ullman House, Oak Park, Illinois;

1905 Wright makes his first trip to Japan with Catherine and clients Mr. and Mrs. Ward Willits; Unity Temple, Oak Park, Illinois

1906 Frederick Robie house, Chicago, Illinois; C. Thaxter Shaw House remodeling, Montreal, Canada

1907 Avery Coonley house, Riverside, Illinois

1909 Wright leaves his family and practice for Europe accompanied by Mamah Borthwick Cheney

1910 Wasmuth publishes monograph of Wright's work: *Ausgeführte Bauten und Entwürfe von Frank Lloyd Wright*

1911 Wright returns to Chicago, then begins design and construction of Taliesin near Spring Green, Wisconsin

1912 Publishes *The Japanese Print*

1913 Wright returns to Japan in pursuit of the Imperial Hotel commission and to purchase more Japanese prints, which he sells; Midway Gardens, Chicago, Illinois

1914 Mamah Cheney is murdered with six others and Taliesin burns; Wright meets Miriam Noel

1915 Wright and Miriam Noel leave for Japan to begin work on the Imperial Hotel

1917 Hollyhock House, Los Angeles, California

1919 Construction begins on the Imperial Hotel, Tokyo, Japan

1922 Wright returns to the United States; his divorce from Catherine is finalized.

1923 The Imperial Hotel survives the great Kanto earthquake of September 1, 1923; Wright marries Miriam Noel

1923–4 The California concrete-block houses: Millard (La Miniatura), Freeman, Storer, Ennis

1924 Noel leaves Wright; Wright meets Olgivanna Milanoff Hinzenburg

1927–8 Wright's series of articles, "In the Cause of Architecture," appears in *The Architectural Record*; Wright is divorced from Miriam Noel

1928 Wright and Olgivanna Hinzenburg are married

1930 Wright delivers the Kahn Lectures at Princeton University

1931 Exhibition of Wright's work opens in Berlin; Wright travels to Rio de Janeiro to serve as judge for the Columbus Memorial Lighthouse competition

1932 Wright's work is included in the Museum of Modern Art's Modern Architecture: International Exhibition; *An Autobiography* and *The Disappearing City* are published; Wright and Olgivanna establish the Taliesin Fellowship

1934 The Taliesin Fellowship begins work on the Broadacre City model

1935 House for Edgar J. Kaufmann, Fallingwater, Bear Run, Pennsylvania

1936 Johnson Wax Company Administration Building and "Wingspread" for Herbert Johnson, Racine, Wisconsin

1937 Wright travels to the Soviet Union for the World Conference of Architects; Herbert Jacobs House, Madison, Wisconsin

1938 Taliesin West, Scottsdale, Arizona

1939 Wright delivers a series of lectures, "An Organic Architecture," in London

1940 Museum of Modern Art Exhibition of Wright's work

1941 Receives the Royal Gold Medal for Architecture from the Royal Institute of British Architects

1943–59 The Solomon R. Guggenheim Museum, New York, New York

1944 Solar Hemicycle for Herbert Jacobs, Middleton, Wisconsin

1949 Receives the Gold Medal of the American Institute of Architects

1951 Exhibition "Sixty Years of Living Architecture"; receives a Gold Medal from the American Academy of Arts and Letters; receives the Star of Solidarity, Venice, Italy

1952 Price Tower for Harold Price, Bartlesville, Oklahoma

1954 Beth Sholom Synagogue, Elkins Park, Pennsylvania

1955 Dallas Theater Center, Dallas Texas

1956 Annunciation Greek Orthodox Church, Wauwatosa, Wisconsin; the Mile High "Illinois" Skyscraper (project)

1957 Plan for Greater Baghdad (project); Marin County Civic Center, Marin County, California

1959 Wright dies in Phoenix, Arizona, on April 9

■

American System: A type of low-cost house design by Frank Lloyd Wright. These were frame houses made of pre-cut lumber and were meant to be assembled at the site.

Architecture: the art and science of designing and constructing buildings.

atrium: An inner court, which may be open to the sky and covered by a roof.

bay: A regular division of the walls, roof, or other part of a building or of the whole building.

bearing wall: A wall that supports the weight of a building rather than one that only divides spaces, such as a partition.

Beaux-Arts style: A rich, nineteenth century revival of classical styles named after the Ecole des Beaux-Arts, an academy of fine arts and architecture in Paris.

Burnham & Root: The Chicago firm of Daniel Burnham (1846–1912) and J.W. Root (1850–1891), which contributed to the development of the Chicago School of architecture. Burnham was chief of construction for the 1893 Chicago World's Fair, where he promoted a revival of the Beaux-Arts style, and later, important early skyscrapers such as the Monadnock Block, Chicago, and the Flatiron Building, New York.

cantilever: A beam supported rigidly at one end to carry a load along the free arm or at the free end. A slanting beam fixed at the base is often used to support the free end, like a bracket. The cantilever design is often used for canopies, and balconies (see pages 82–83, 86).

The Chicago School of architecture: The group of Chicago architects who established a style of modern commercial architecture. It began with the introduction of steel-frame construction by William Le Baron Jenney (1832–1907), and continued with the work of Holabird & Roche, Burnham & Root, Adler & Sullivan, and Frank Lloyd Wright.

Chicago World's Fair (World's Columbian Exposition of 1893): An exhibition of technology and the arts at which Chicago's leading architectural firms exhibited. As a result, the city became a leading architectural center.

classicism: A revival of, or return to, the principles of ancient Greek or Roman art and architecture.

dendriform: Resembling a tree in structure (see pages 92–93, 95).

draftsman: One who executes construction drawings for an architect.

"form follows function": Louis H. Sullivan's architectural motto, by which he meant that the form of a structure should reflect its purpose. *See functionalism.*

foundation: The bottommost part of a structure; it rests in or on the supporting earth.

functionalism: The belief that the function of a building is of primary importance, and that its design must not interfere with its purpose, and should reflect that purpose.

gable: The top, triangular part of the end wall of a building, formed by a sloping roof.

gothic: The architecture of the thirteenth, fourteenth, and fifteenth centuries in Europe, most often seen in the great cathedrals; it was built of stone and characterized in part by pointed arches and high vaulted ceilings.

Walter Gropius: (1883–1969) German-American architect, and one of the founders of modern functional architecture. He was the director of the Weimar Arts and Crafts School, which he reorganized and renamed as the Bauhaus. This became a movement devoted to the notion that all the plastic arts—sculpture, painting, design, and handicrafts—should be united into a new architecture.

Holabird & Roche: The Chicago firm of William Holabird (1854–1923) and Martin Roche (1855–1927) that was instrumental in establishing steel-skeleton skyscraper construction, later to be known as the Chicago School of architecture.

Internationalists: Proponents of the early modern International style of architecture.

International style: A term coined in the United States in the 1930s to refer to the new architectural style created before World War I by such architects as Wright, Gropius, and others. The style is characterized by general cubic shapes and lighter mass, often resulting in an unembellished framework surrounding great expanses of glass.

leaded glass: Stained-glass panels separated by narrow lead dividers.

Le Corbusier, pseudonym of Charles Édouard Jeanneret: (1887–1965) French architect whose buildings and writings had a revolutionary effect on the development of modern architecture. He conceived of the house as a "machine for living," elements of which included raising it off the ground on pillars, providing roof gardens and strip windows, and an open plan.

masonry: Any earthen building material such as brick, tile, or stone that is held together by mortar.

medieval: Characteristic of the Middle Ages, which extended from the fifth to the fourteenth centuries in Europe.

Ludwig Mies van der Rohe: (1886–1969) German-American architect, who is one of the founders of modern architecture. He is most famous for designing all-glass skyscrapers with steel structural frames in Chicago and New York in the 1920s through the 1950s.

open plan: A type of interior plan with a minimum of partitions between rooms, which was made possible by the use of columns rather than walls to bear the weight of the structure.

organic architecture: Architecture seen as an active element of living rather than a reflection or embellishment of life.

polychrome: Decorated with several colors.

Prairie House: A type of home Wright built in the early 1900s. In it, Wright tried to reduce the number of separate rooms and make all come together as a unified space; to associate the building with its site by keeping it close to the ground; to get rid of the basement and bring it above ground; and to make furnishings that would conform to the house's style. He also made the hearth the focal point of the interior, reflecting his views on how the ideal family should live. The Prairie School consists of those architects that followed Wright's initial design idea (see pages 44–45).

scaffold: A temporary structure that supports platforms aiding workmen in construction.

shingle style: An American style, usually applied to medium-sized private houses, whose primary characteristics are open internal planning and the use of wooden shingles as an all-over external wall covering.

steel: Iron combined with varying amounts of carbon to provide the varying degrees of hardness and elasticity needed in construction.

steel-frame construction: A method used in building skyscrapers, developed in the late 1890s and early 1900s, which involves having a steel skeleton bear the weight of a building rather than external masonry walls. This development permitted the development of taller, lighter buildings.

Louis H. Sullivan: (1856–1924) A partner in the Chicago firm of Adler & Sullivan, Sullivan was of great importance in the evolution of modern architecture in the United States. His dominating principle was that outward form should express the function of a building. He was against the revival of classicism that was popular at the time and instead advocated the establishment of an architecture that should be functional and also truly American.

textile block construction: A method of construction, which Wright invented and first used in four homes built in Los Angeles between 1917 and 1924. The textile blocks are small cast-concrete shells, held together by a network of steel rods grouted into the shells on site, and assembled to form double walls with a central cavity. The weaving of the steel rods inspired the name. The blocks could be decorated or plain and the cavity could hold ducts or flues. Sometimes they were pierced to allow air or light to pass through (see pages 56–57).

Usonian House: A type of inexpensive house design by Frank Lloyd Wright, which he felt reflected the American style of living. Generally, the design consisted of laying down a concrete platform with heating pipes cast in. The concrete would be mixed with red coloring to give a warm, earthy cast to the interiors. On this were erected a brick core around the kitchen and one or two other brick supporting screens. The roof was flat, supported by the brick walls, and was higher over the living-dining area, lower over the bedrooms. Toward the garden, the windows were often floor-to-ceiling doors (see page 87).

■

BIBLIOGRAPHY

Primary Sources on the architect and his life

Barney, Maginel Wright, *Valley of the God-Almighty Joneses*, Appleton Century, New York, 1965. Wright's younger sister places Wright's life and work within the context of the Lloyd-Jones clan.

Tafel, Edgar, *Years With Frank Lloyd Wright: Apprentice to Genius*, McGraw Hill, New York, 1979, reissued by Dover, 1985. Recollections of a Taliesin Fellow (1932–1941).

Wright, Frank Lloyd, *Frank Lloyd Wright Collected Writings*, Bruce Brooks Pfeiffer (editor), Volume 1, 1894–1930 (1992); Volume II, 1930–32, Rizzoli, New York. Volume II contains the original version of *An Autobiography*, the ultimate source for information on Wright's life, although it should be read in conjunction with secondary literature that describes Wright's occasional deviations from the empirical facts.

Wright, John Lloyd, *My Father, Frank Lloyd Wright*, Dover, New York, 1992 (originally *My Father Who Is on Earth*, 1946). Reminiscences by the architect's son.

Wright, Olgivanna Lloyd, *Frank Lloyd Wright, His Life His Work His Words*, Horizon Press, New York, 1966. Olgivanna's story. Contains extensive transcripts of Wright's talks to the Taliesin Fellowship.

References books on Wright

Kaufmann, Edgar J., Jr., *Nine Commentaries on Frank Lloyd Wright*, M.I.T. Press, Boston, 1989.

Pfeiffer, Bruce Brooks (text), Peter Gossel and Gabriele Leuthauser (editors), *Frank Lloyd Wright*, Taschen, Koln, Germany, 1991. Pictures and descriptions of Wright buildings.

Pfeiffer, Bruce Brooks, *Frank Lloyd Wright Drawings: Masterworks from the Frank Lloyd Wright Archives*, Harry N. Abrams, New York, 1990.

Storrer, William, *The Architecture of Frank Lloyd Wright: A Complete Catalog*, M.I.T. Press, Boston, 1974. An indispensable catalog of every known building designed by Wright.

Storrer, William, *Frank Lloyd Wright; A Guide to Extant Structures*, WAS Productions, Newark, 1991. A supplement to Storrer's *Catalog*, maps and directions to extant Wright structures.

Sweeney, Robert, *Frank Lloyd Wright: An Annotated Bibliography*, Hennessey & Ingalls, Inc., Los Angeles, 1978. An invaluable guide to Wright's published work, and works about Wright through 1977.

Biographies

Gill, Brendan, *Many Masks: A Life of Frank Lloyd Wright*, Ballantine Books, New York, 1987. An irreverent demythologizing of Wright who, Gill argues, during his life constructed "many masks" to hide his insecurities.

Secrest, Meryle, *Frank Lloyd Wright*, Alfred Knopf, New York, 1992. A celebration of the great artist, which emphasizes the scandals that surrounded Wright's life.

Twombly, Robert C, *Frank Lloyd Wright, His Life and His Architecture*, John Wiley and Sons, New York, 1987. A thorough discussion of Wright's philosophy and his architecture.

Books on Wright's architecture

Hitchcock, Henry Russell, *In the Nature of Materials: The Buildings of Frank Lloyd Wright 1887–1941*, Da Capo Publications, New York, 1975. The definitive work on Wright's architecture to 1941.

O'Gorman, James, *Three American Architects: Richardson, Sullivan, and Wright*, University of Chicago Press, 1991. The architects who influenced Wright.

Smith, Norris Kelly, *Frank Lloyd Wright: A Study in Architectural Content*, Prentice Hall, 1979. Argues that Wright's architecture was primarily conservative, not radical, in nature.

General books on twentieth-century American architecture

Blake, Peter, *The Master Builders: Le Corbusier, Mies van der Rohe, Frank Lloyd Wright*, W.W. Norton, New York, 1976.

Frampton, Kenneth, *Modern Architecture: A Critical History*, Thames and Hudson Ltd., London and New York, Third Edition, 1992.

Jackson, Kenneth T., *Crabgrass Frontier: The Suburbanization of the United States*, Oxford University Press, New York, 1985.

Jencks, Charles, *Modern Movements in Architecture*, Viking Penguin, New York, 1987.

Jordy, William H. *American Buildings and Their Architects: Volume Four, Progressive and Academic Ideals at the Turn of the Twentieth Century*, Oxford University Press, 1986.

■

INDEX